CROSSINGS ON A BRIDGE OF LIGHT

CROSSINGS ON A BRIDGE OF LIGHT

*The Songs and Deeds of Gesar, King of Ling, As He Travels to
Shambhala Through the Realms of Life and Death*

DOUGLAS J. PENICK

Mountain Treasury Press
1850 Folsom St #606
Boulder, Colorado 80302

ISBN-13 : 978-0974597430
ISBN-10: 0974597430

TABLE OF CONTENTS

INTRODUCTION

The Gesar epic is a vast body of literature that recounts the struggles of Gesar Norbu Dradul, the legendary 12th century King of Ling in Eastern Tibet. Gesar was renowned for the many battles and quests he undertook to secure the wellbeing, prosperity and peace of his beleaguered kingdom, and he came to be regarded as the embodiment of continuous cultural and spiritual renewal.

In all his endeavors, Gesar is inspired by fearless compassion. Unafraid of chaos, he is able to uncover a path of wakefulness and harmony even in the most perilous and compromising situations. His unconditional commitment to others gives birth to the confidence that always uncovers spontaneous, precise and vital expressions of enlightened mind. Thus, he is revered throughout central Asia in Buddhist, Shambhala and shamanic teachings as the perfect warrior.

The Spirit of Renewal

Gesar's character in all his journeys is somewhat unique in Asian folklore. He is, even before his birth, an enlightened being. However he is also a classic epic hero, prey to a range of flaws. Unlike the Buddha who, having once realized enlightenment, was invulnerable to worldly sorrows and blandishments, Gesar is repeatedly caught in nets of outer and inner conflict. He repeatedly engages his torment and confusion in order to uncover the freedom of fundamental wakefulness.

The deepest impulse in the Gesar tradition is the constant renewal of enlightenment in the world. It is this dynamic—the constant rediscovery of wakefulness and compassion within the most horrific, grotesque, and frightening situations—that accounts for the Gesar epic's continued vitality in its many elaborations.

A Living Tradition

One of the world's most extensive bodies of epic lore, the Gesar songs and stories have long focused the social and spiritual aspirations of Eastern Tibet, Western China, Mongolia, Buryatsia, and the Kalmuk Republic. This epic tradition is still alive, in a wide variety of forms, today.

Itinerant Gesar singers perpetuate the saga's basic episodes and characters in improvised songs and chants, with some illiterate singers pretending to recite from written texts, and others unfurling scrolls that depict the tales of their songs. In eastern Tibet and elsewhere, an elaborate theatrical tradition boasts distinctive dances, costumes, and backdrops.

The epic has also been composed in written form, most famously in the early 20th century at the behest of Ju Mipham Rinpoche, the great Nyingma lama and scholar. This written tradition includes many liturgies invoking Gesar as a deity, protector, and spiritual guide. Of the written versions now available to us from Tibet,

Mongolia, and Ladakh, many were adapted in whole or in part from the songs and performances of one or more singers. Meanwhile new episodes have continued to appear in response to the inspiration and needs of the time. One lama, for example, hearing of the horrors of World War Two, composed an episode in which Gesar went to Germany to conquer Hitler.

The Gesar epic is unlike the *Mahabharata*, which exists in one definitive written form, or the *Ramayana* which exists in two. Throughout India and Southeast Asia, the many theatrical and spiritual variations of these two great Indian epics assume the stability of the root texts. By contrast, the Gesar epic is constantly evolving, as are its modes of presentation (with some songs and performances containing only selected episodes). In this sense, it is very much a living, improvisatory tradition. Because its message continues to inspire people in many cultures to find courage and hope in the hardships they encounter daily, new renditions of the Gesar epic have often arisen in times of special uncertainty and danger.

The Heart of the Story
The Gesar Epic has a core repertoire of episodes. These include Gesar's celestial origin and miraculous birth, his childhood and accession to the throne, his four great campaigns against the demonic lords of the four directions, and his departure from this earth. Other episodes tell of his battles in foreign lands, undertaken to procure various spiritual and material riches for the people of Ling. (These can be found in Rolf Stein's work, Alexandra David Neel's Superhuman Life of Gesar of Ling, Douglas Penick's Warrior Song of King Gesar, and the late Robin Kornman's forthcoming translation, among others.)

The episode recounted in this book is also part of the traditional canon, but less well known and it tells of Gesar's journey to rescue his mother from hell. To do so, Gesar, after encountering the great protectors Vajrasadhu and Vetali, enters the kingdom of Yama, Lord of Death (part 1) he then travels through the six realms of existence and the interim states or bardos (part2). And afterwards, he visits the Kingdom of Shambhala, where he meets four great warrior rulers who frame this journey in a worldly societal context (part 3). Finally, (in part 4), King Gesar makes his last return to Ling.

This episode is in some ways the epitome of all Gesar's other endeavors. Here he experiences each of the six realms of being: hell, the realm of hungry ghosts, animals, humans, jealous gods, and gods. These realms are traditional in Tibetan, Indian and other central Asian cosmologies, but even as they may be considered 'real' places, they also represent the kinds of worlds that evolve from our own states of mind. Thus, when our anger becomes completely solid, our world becomes an all-encompassing source of pain; when our craving becomes incessant, we inhabit a world of utter deprivation; willful ignorance makes a world of endless apprehension; clinging to stability accentuates a world of constant change; envy produces a world where what is most desired is in the possession of others; and the hallucinations of self-absorption flourish in complete indifference. From this point of view, we may find that all these realms not just resonate but even exist in our human world.

At the same time, the actual experiences of anger, craving, ignoring and so forth are all intensely, even unsparingly alive. We try to harness them to our narrative of a solid self who achieves goals in a solid world. But, letting go of such reference points, the very energy of the passions becomes a path of enlightenment. Passions awaken us to what is real in the world, in ourselves, in life, in dying. Thus, Gesar's experience of each realm leads him to realize the immediate enlightenment there.

Although in this rendition, the six realms and the Buddhas within them are represented traditionally, this story lives beyond its original cultural framework. The inner truth of Gesar's journey is not ultimately confined to any specific imagery. The demonic figures are expressions of our own inner terrors; the Buddhas (literally: 'awakened ones') refer to the intrinsic clarity and vividness of our own minds. Beyond any specific cultural or spiritual tradition, Gesar continues to provoke and inspire because we continually sense that there is an intensity, a truthfulness beyond our own limitations, and we continue to dare to seek it, even beyond the limits of life and death.

*

As this entire episode has never been translated into English, I have relied on the Gesar tradition as transmitted to me by the Vidyadhara, the Venerable Chogyam Trungpa, Rinpoche, the Dorje Dradul of Mukpo Dong. I have also been given unstinting and generous assistance from the teachings of His Holiness Orgyen Kusum Lingpa, the Venerable Tulku Thondup, the Venerable Chagdud Tulku Rinpoche, the Venerable Yangthang Tulku, and the Venerable Namkhai Drimed Rinpoche. I am also deeply indebted to Ives Waldo, the late Robin Kornman, Blake Thomson, and the works of R.A. Stein, Alexandra David Neel, Ida Zeitlin, and Geoffrey Samuels.

DJP
Boulder, Colorado
11/11/08

INVOCATION CALLING ON GESAR KING OF LING

i

Now when the virtues of the human realm
Wane like a sallow moon drowning in a molten copper sea,
The phantasmagoria of the six realms pollute the air
And take possession of the human mind.

Civilization collapses, societies implode
On teeming battlegrounds of pain and fear.
Armies of tormented Hell Beings swell and rage
As tribes and clans are turned to murderous mobs
Ravaging their ancient lands, uprooting all.

So severed from established human bonds,
Pressed on by their insatiable appetites,
Men and women scour the earth like Hungry Ghosts,
Devouring elders, daughters, friends, lovers, parents, sons
To fill their inner emptiness.

Words lose meaning. There are no norms.
Culture is now a din of venal exhortation,
Wisdom is now the lost opinions of the dead.
Like beasts, all shut their minds
And hide deep in the migrations of the herd.

Claustrophobia and uncontrollable fate
Mock the ways all know and wish to know themselves,
And many, like jealous gods denied their birthright,
Plot incessantly to seize knowledge, wealth and power
To rise above the sorrows of the world.

The fortunate aspire only to dwell untroubled
In a vast expanse of light,
Absorbed in infinite arrays of fabricated bliss,
And like the radiant gods of desire form and formlessness,
Live eternally in utter indifference,
In indomitable peace.

So having lost confidence in our own humanity.
So having ravaged the earth to sustain our dreams,
So having debased truth and true love,
Can we still yearn to discover the virtues of the human realm?

Hounded by suffering and the specter of death,
We cry out for the great warrior within us to arise.

ii

King Lion Gesar, Crest Jewel of Warriors,
Vajra Subduer of Maras, Protector of the Human Realm,
Heart of Dharma and Deathless Lord of Life,
You stand amid clouds of hosts of Drala and Werma,
Like the noon-day sun at the summit of the six realms.
To whom can we now look but you?

Please come to us now in this stricken world
Where we twist in nets of delusion and pain.
Please restore the virtues of this human realm.

Come, wearing the pristine golden armor of confidence,
Brandishing the razor sword of wisdom
And your meteoric arrows of compassion.
Come mounted on your great horse of miracles, Kyang Ko Kar Kar.
Lion Lord Norbu Dradul, Gesar King of Ling,
Flying through the air with your vast retinue of warriors
Shouting KI and SO,
Come to us here and now.

Grasp the Mu cord that joins heaven and earth.
Grasp the Mu cord that passes through life and death.
Grasp the Mu cord that joins the time of legend with the present.
Descend on our offering of billowing juniper smoke.
Accept this offering of our pure longing.
Restore the virtues of this human realm.

From the kingdom of no dharma,
Come into our hearts
As the signless expanse of primordial awareness.

From the spontaneity of authentic presence,
Come into our perceptions
As a blazing rainbow of wisdom light.

From the equanimity of Dharmadhatu,
Fill our beings
With confidence untouched by bias.

As space, as light, as compassion;
As a gap, as a shout, as a story, as a living being—
Be with us here and now
Restore the heart of this human realm.

Show us the way through the realms of life and death.
Show what does not change in the endless sea of change.
And while time remains, live in our hearts
As the light of our true being.

Penetrating the darkness of painful illusion,
Show the dawn of Vajrasattva,
The luminous bridge through the six realms and three times.

Show us the path within the human heart
To the Kingdom of Shambhala here and now.

When the future seems most perilous and there is no clear refuge, when the truth has degenerated into a logic of advantage, when teachers are self-seeking, when friends and loved ones are fickle, when sickness, danger, death, or battle looms; at such a time this invocation to Gesar, Norbu Dradul, is sung. With offerings of billowing juniper smoke and the music of cymbals, it is sung in a strong melodious voice.

PART 1
HALUCINATIONS OF SORROW

The story begins as Gesar falls prey to restless anguish. His sister, the goddess Manene, then comes to him and sings of their mother's entrapment in hell. Gesar goes into solitary retreat and meets the Dharma Protector Vajrasadhu. While outwardly appearing to have fallen into a coma, Gesar journeys to the edge of life, only to encounter the Great Vetali. These deeds and songs are set forth here.

After many years of war and battle, the All Victorious Warrior, Gesar Lion Lord of Ling looks out on a kingdom that is peaceful, prosperous and secure. The seasons sweep down from snow-capped mountain peaks and move in splendor across the green and golden plains. Harvests are plentiful. Herds of yaks and horses flourish. Children are born and grow strong in the Buddhist and Shambhala disciplines. Lay teachers and lay practitioners keep the spiritual life of the kingdom strong. This way of life is now deeply rooted. And now, when people think back on the many battles fought to bring them to their current state, they shiver to think of the rigors in such harsh and unsettled times.

The Demon Lords of the Four Directions were long ago suppressed. Lutzen is no more than dust; the Horpa were extinguished, imprisoned, or tamed: Satham of Jang and King Shingti no longer poisoned the earth. There are no more enemies. Yet the mind of Gesar, Lion King of Ling is apprehensive; his body is stiff and tense.

*

Gesar's Unease
Often now, Gesar is caught in waves of inexplicable sadness from which nothing can distract him. Feasts, horse races, archery contests, philosophical debate seem hollow. The company of beautiful and clever women provides no solace. Even meditation

now tires him easily. Every effort to ease his mind leaves him more anxious. Though all he has been born to do is done, he feels no peace. The vague sense that he has missed something crucial troubles him, but he can not discover what it is.

In the brittle chill when winter has begun to weaken but spring has not yet come, Gesar rides out on his Horse of Wind, Kyang Ko Kar Kar. They canter across the rolling plains of Ling, far from any dwelling or herdsman's path. And as he rides, he looks into the pearl gray sky and sings:

Ah,
The white cranes with long red legs
Soar northward through the empty sky.
Their cry of greeting shakes the cold air,
But they fly on and do not stop here.
What are the winds that carry them?

They leave behind their warm blue lakes,
Warm breezes, green canopies of trees,
As they abandon jeweled palaces in the South.
What are the winds that carry them?

Ah
The white cranes with long red legs
Soar Northward through the empty sky.
Their cry of greeting shakes the cold air,
But they fly on and do not stop here.

They fly to the frozen steppe beside a frozen sea.
There beneath a silver sky,
They will raise their wings and long red legs in dance
And draw the spring up through the ice.
Who showed them this ancient dance?

Ah
The white cranes with long red legs
Soar northward through the empty sky.
Their cry of greeting shakes the cold air,
But they fly on and do not stop here.
What are the winds that carry them?

Faithful to the cycles of what enduring love,
Why do they call to me?
Who taught them this ancient song?

One cold night, Gesar wakes suddenly, shaken by a dream that vanishes the minute he opens his eyes. His head aches. He rises in confusion, leaves his tent, and walks into the foothills. As he strides upward on a rocky path, the villages below dissolve in darkness. Beneath the pale light of a half moon, the vast plain of Ling is enveloped in a sea of luminous mist. Only the faint echo of a child's sudden cry, the muffled stirring of horses and the lowing of yaks hint that Ling exists. Gesar sits down on a cold rock outcropping within a shallow glade of juniper trees. Above him the half moon glows within a frozen haze.

From that mist, slowly and silently, Gesar's sister, the goddess Manene appears before him. Her hair is black as midnight and her face pale as the winter moon. Her black silk robe adorned with seas of constellations swirls softly on the air, and her eyes shine like twin crescent moons. Staring gravely at Gesar, she smiles and, with a voice like a sharp breeze from the distant northern steppes, she sings this song to him.

*

Manene Sings of a Mother Trapped in Hell

Hail Brother, Regent of the Rigden Kings,
Protector of the human realm, Lord of a thousand tents.
You are the conqueror of all fears and evils
Seen and known within this world.

Your confidence is immovable as a mountain range.
Your wisdom is inseparable from light itself.
Your wakefulness is uninterrupted as the sky.
But now the solid-seeming ground of being,
Your history and your world,
Cracks beneath you.
The tides of universal hallucination
Roar beneath your feet.

Safe and secure, the hearts of the warriors of Ling
Are growing small and complacent.
Safe and secure, the minds of the spiritual practitioners of Ling
Are seeking to escape the turmoil of life and death.
Chaos, terror, pain, sacrifice and loss seem all so long ago.

The true path of warriorship
And true way of spiritual practice
Are being lost in pretension, nostalgia,
Intellectual learning and empty ritual.
Chaos, terror, pain, sacrifice and loss seem all so long ago.

But now the solid-seeming ground of being,
Your history and your world,
Cracks beneath you.
The tides of universal hallucination
Roar beneath your feet.

Now only the vast heart of compassion,
The deep heartbeat of true love
Can be relied upon.
Now, most dear and beloved brother,
Great heart, great being,
There is nothing else.
Now as the solid-seeming ground of being
Cracks beneath you.
You must dive into the tides of universal hallucination
That roar beneath your feet.

Then Manene reaches up with her right hand, seizes the bright half moon. She turns it over and holds it out to him like a vast silver bowl. Inside is a trembling lake of mercury. The silvery liquid begins to spin and slowly forms a shimmering whirlpool, racing ever faster, roaring and opening downward into the depth of emptiness. As if he were seized by a tornado, Gesar is dragged down into a black pulsing void.

Suddenly Gesar finds himself on a high rock promontory, dressed in golden armor, the satin pennants of his crystal helmet snapping in the wind, his crystal sword unsheathed, his bow and arrows ready, sitting astride his sleek horse of miracles, Kyang Ko Kar Kar. Below, sinking deep into the earth is a dark abyss from which stinking vapors and tortured wails rise up on gusts of burning air.

Gesar peers down into the chasm and sees that it is filled with human beings. Men and women of all ages and descriptions, all with great pack loads on their raw and bleeding backs, struggle to climb out of this pit whose walls are made of boiling mud. Each crawls up one step, slides back, is trod on by another. Those above kick the faces and arms of those below, who, in turn, claw and bite at those above. Desperate to escape, all scream and curse as they are beaten, scalded, and choked with slides of burning rotten mud.

Gesar stares into the seething foul mass of tortured beings. Shocked beyond speech, suddenly he sees his mother Dzeden, so long lost to him. She is lying on her back, kicking at those below her, crying, while trying to grasp the shins of one above. Geysers of burning pitch erupt beneath her. The flesh on her chest and stomach are shredded and raw. The flesh and bones of her arms and legs are charred black. Boiling mud courses down her face which is a mask of horror etched on an exposed skull.

With a great shout Gesar and his fearless horse fly down into the reeking pit, and hover there before his mother's mad uncomprehending gaze. Gesar looks at her and sobs, but cannot speak. Slowly a look of understanding enters his mother's eyes and in a cracked voice, she sings to him.

"Oh my son, my son,
For many lifetimes now, it has been my only wish
To see your face once more.

When first we parted,
I saw you in the face of strangers
And heard your voice in the whispers of the wind.
A falling branch would be your footstep,
And when crowds gathered in the market,
I thought they were gossiping about your return.

But then the great Hor army swept through Ling.
You were not there, and no place was safe.
I slipped away, dressed as a beggar pilgrim,
Avoiding your enemies and treacherous kinsmen.

Though I had no food and snow began to fall,
I made my way back to the deserted valley
Where I raised you as a child.
Exhausted by cold and the long journey,
Starving and delirious,
I fell beside a frozen stream.
The ice was smooth and black,
And I saw a face:
An old hag whom I scarcely recognized.
When I realized that this face was mine,
I wept and my tears were the only warmth I felt for many days.

I remembered that once I had been a Naga Princess.
I was beautiful; my night-black hair billowed like a cloud.
My gold crown was adorned with pearls and opals;
My coral-colored skirts were softer than any man-made silk.
I danced and flew in my home beneath the sea.
My laughter echoed like a tinkling bell
Through the great Naga capital Bhogavati, City of Pleasure.
And I was loved by my father, Vasuki,
Who ruled over every shining sea, lake, and stream
From this joyful city beneath the banks of the Ganges.
There my mother, kin, and court enfolded me
In boundless love and every form of happiness.
Pain was unknown to me.
You do not remember.

But then I became like this, a dried up stick;
My hair scant and gray, my clothes rags,
And it seemed centuries since I had laughed.
Only one thing redeemed my years of sorrow and betrayal:
That is you, my much-loved Gesar.
You alone brought the light of joy
Into this world of endless pain.
Do you remember?

And with that thought, breath left my body.
My love for you, dear son,
And my body that bore and suckled you
Split apart.
There was no one to close the eyes of the corpse
That had been me.
My body, unburied, rotted
As the stream melted and flowed,
Sparkling and rushing to the Kingdom of Ling.
My mind, thinking only to see your face again,
Entered that stream and took the form of a rainbow trout.

And glimpse you I did.
Re-entering Ling one day at dawn,
Wearing your sun-like golden armor,
Your helmet of crystal with fluttering pennants,

Carrying your lightning sword,
And riding on the gleaming horse of miracles,
Kyang Ko Karkar,
You forded a stream.
You were laughing.

Looking up for an instant, I saw you.
I leapt out of the water.
You, racing onward, did not see.
And I could not linger.
The racing torrent carried me along.
How could you remember this?

A golden eagle soon after sunk his claws into my side,
Lifted me, gasping, high into the air then
Dropped, killed and consumed me.
So, to see you again, I took the form
Of that greatest and most powerful of hunting birds.
And many times, as I circled through the thin air
Of the cool morning sky, I did see you
Riding out to battle with your warrior companions
Across the golden plains of Ling,
Meeting in counsel with your ministers,
Leaving the tent of a lover in the night,
Walking alone, and sitting in solitude.
I sorrowed at seeing you only from afar.
I flew too close.
One man sought to impress you with his skill at archery.
His iron arrow pierced my neck.
With all my strength, I flew straight up,
Calling out your name as I rose.
High where there is no longer air
But only light: I fell.
Do you remember this?

I became a warrior in your army
When you fought against Satham of Jang.
I was young and inexperienced
But I shadowed you everywhere.
A champion of Jang rode up behind you,

Intent on severing your head from your body with his curved sword.
Calling out you name, I came between you and him,
And so lost my life.
Do you remember this?

And on it went through forms and lives
I can barely recall:
Insect, dog, maiden, horse—oh, on and on.
And oh, you who are a hero,
How would you remember
Or know me anymore?
Unhappy in so many forms,
The memory of the happy Princess
Whom once I was remained.
I thirsted for pure water and hungered for choice food,
But all before me became rotten and poisonous.
I was a ghost flying madly from place to place.
I thought on how my life
In the glimmering beauty of the Naga realm
Had been changed.
And by whom, and by what method, and for what aim?

This story is part of your legend,
And it echoes like a drumbeat in my mind.
Though surely you have heard it many times.
I cannot help but tell it once again.

Not so long ago, due to an evil daughter's curse,
A great evil was set loose upon the earth.
Rage, greed, lust, and fear
Threatened to poison the hearts of human-kind.
Warfare, famine, disease and oppression
Were soon to dominate the lives of all.

So did Padmasambhava set out to bring a great warrior
Into this world of men and women,
To conquer the demonic lords,
To be an exemplar and guide,
To be the Lion Lord, Gesar of Ling,
To be you.

In order that you not be completely subject
To these demons' calls,
You needed a Naga mother of royal birth.
Padmasambhava selected me
But my turquoise-scaled father
Who, from his pearl encrusted turquoise throne
Ruled a hundred oceans and a thousand seas,
Would not let me go.

Padmasambhava then poisoned the water of our seas.
The Naga race fell ill. Many died.
I was the price for Padmasambhava's cure.

So was I delivered by my weeping family
Into the human realm so rich in suffering.
There, amid your family, I lived a servant's life,
Was reviled, abused, exiled, and died.

Though this memory causes constant pain,
I cannot turn away from it.
Dwelling on this story,
I came to hate the name and form of Padmasambhava,
Revered throughout the three worlds as a Second Buddha.

It was due to him alone
That I, a joyful princess, free and loved,
Became a slave to every shift of fate and fortune.

My mind flew between longing for you
And hatred of the Guru Rinpoche.
I could find no further truth and found no rest.

So I was carried on a raging wind
Through a swirl of joys and horrors,
As if I were a being of light, a being of resentment,
A being of hunger, a being of loss,
A being of wrath, of stillness, of envy, of sorrow,
Desire, yearning, terror, regret.

I dwelt in worlds composed of burning gas,
In worlds of knives, in worlds of flowered scent,
In worlds of crushing density, of jewel light,
In seas of endless satisfactions just out of reach.

In this relentless and unceasing swirl,
Caught in the oscillation of nightmares and dreams
I forgot who I was.
Absorbed completely in intensity,
Moving, moving,
I forgot all whys, wheres, and hows.
I forgot you.

Until now
When suddenly in this place,
I see you,
Your face, you once more.

Here you are real
And all else is dream.
I laugh and I cry.
I remember.

Oh,
I beg you now, my beloved son,
I beg you Gesar,
If love is in your heart for me still,
Take me from this place.

I am in Hell.
Take me home and set me free."

But before he can respond or call to her, Gesar loses consciousness. He wakes lying on the cold ground in the frozen dark. He does not know how much time has passed. The moon has set and the only light comes from the hard glitter of distant stars. Before his eyes, the image of his sister dissolves in a luminous mist that hovers in the nearby juniper trees. He smells sandalwood, hears the swish of silk. He hears her faint melodious voice sing once more.

Manene's song is sung in a delicate lyrical voice and is accompanied by dance.

Now, Gesar, Hero of a thousand battles,
Conqueror of a thousand kinds of corruption,
Healer of a thousand kinds of poisonous disease,
Now you cannot turn back.

Now the accomplishments, realizations and victories,
Which you called your life are behind you.

Now the living heart of compassion
Draws you out and onward.

To save a single being,
You will experience the loss of death,
Your body and mind dissolve.

To save a single being,
You will go beyond your identity,
Your body, your understanding, your life.

You will experience again the painful uncertainty of birth,
As your mind and body dissolve
And form a being you have never known.

The awakened state cannot be contained in body or word or thought.
It is continually renewed in the endless cycles of birth and death.
The transitions of the bardos are the path of wakefulness.

As all life is sustained by other,
Only complete compassion
Can sustain you.
This is the only ground.

Primordial compassion is unfabricated awareness.
Samaya.
Non-Dual compassion is unchanging bliss.
Samaya.
Unceasing compassion is the all protecting armor of love.
Samaya.

Unconditional confidence is the radiance of compassion.
Samaya.
This is the feast of phenomenal existence.
Samaya.
SAMAYA JA

Suddenly Gesar is overwhelmed by exhaustion. As the pink edge of dawn shines behind the eastern mountains and smoke begins to rise from the tents below, he returns to his home.

*

Gesar's Miraculous Encounters During his Retreat
Now the story is told of Gesar's retreat and his meeting with the Dharma Protector Vajrasadhu, the spontaneous presence of living dharmata.

Gesar lies down in his tent; his body feels ever more heavy and inert. By night, slumber does not restore him, and his sleep is filled with obscure dreams that leave him depleted. By day, he wanders as if asleep. A child playing with a toy bow and arrow, a youth cantering on a horse, a young girl reading, women chatting, men laughing, an old widow warming herself in the sun, all seem puppets animated by forces they do not know, parading on a stage whose fragility they cannot imagine.

Gesar's feverish distraction makes his friends uneasy. When the people of Ling see him so distressed, they become hesitant. A feeling of depression begins to pervade the air. His wife, Sechan Dugmo is also apprehensive, and she lashes out angrily: "What do you think you are doing? Do you think you have no responsibilities? Do you think you can just die?"

"I still care for all of you," Gesar replies wearily, "But what do you want me to do? What?"

Sechan Dugmo can find nothing more to say and, shaking her head, leaves him alone. Secretly she writes to Gesar's most trusted advisers to see what they can do, and one by one they visit him. First comes the general, Chopa Tongden who had fought by his side in every battle. Bluff and taciturn, Chopa Tongden can find no words to rouse his lord. Then comes Norbu Chopel to whom Gesar had confided his spiritual teachings. He can only repeat to Gesar things that he had learned from him. Familiar words have no effect. Finally the Prime Minister, Tseshang Denma visits, but even he, renowned for his tact and diplomacy, cannot penetrate Gesar's black mood.

As if a shadow is rising within him, Gesar secretly feels he is dying. His body and world are slowly dissolving like a bright sunset cloud fading into a night sky. All he has struggled to accomplish and has actually achieved seems like a dream. His wife, his ministers and friends are increasingly remote; their words and sentiments predictable and hollow. Children and young people, so full of life, curiosity and idealism seem sadly and inescapably deluded. Everything will vanish when Yama, Lord of Death pulls the puppets off the stage and strikes the set. No accomplishment, however noble, generous, grand, or good, can alter this.

Finally Gesar decides to go on retreat. He appoints his nephew, Odkar Gyaltsen, to rule in his stead, and many are relieved. But no one knew where he intends to go and for how long he will stay.

On a bleak foggy dawn, Gesar's wife, his heir, his ministers and warriors assemble to bid him farewell and to hear whatever advice he might offer. But as he sits on his great steed, he can only stare silently into the eyes of each, one by one. And each turns away, for meeting his gaze is like looking into a black fathomless pool.

Gesar leaves, riding Kyang Ko Kar Kar and carrying only the simplest supplies. He travels night and day, through blizzard and blinding sun until he reaches the desert valley on the eastern border of Ling where he and his mother lived in exile many years before. There, in a small cave on the side of a sandstone bluff, he makes camp and builds a lean-to to protect the wonder horse from snow and hail.

Looking out over the ice-glazed snowy plain, Gesar sits unmoving for many days staring into the pale horizonless space before him. He watches sadly as the watery sun rises and sets, the pallid moon moves through her cycles, and the stars glitter faintly, drifting on their secret paths.

"Ho, Great Hero," snorts the miracle horse on a breath of steam, "Aside from creating a wasteland with your black mood, what is our purpose here? Now even deer and wild beasts do not show themselves. Mice do not dare peep from their holes, and owls do not dare to hoot. What great enemy will we next subdue?" Gesar sighs, and sings softly.

From the shining heart of enlightenment itself,
From the eternal wakefulness of the natural state,
I came into this world.

I came into this world to quell the demons
Who twist, torture and delude the human mind.
There is no battle I have not won.
There is no terror that I have not overcome.

But I have been like a child
Playing on the frozen surface of a raging stream,
A fish who thinks he swims freely
When he is already caught in a razor net;

A rat feeding in a baited trap.
Whether I stay or leave,
This will not change.

Every being I have ever seen,
Ever loved, ever fought against, or known,
Whatever their wisdom, love, or gallantry,
Is but a cog in an invincible mill
Grinding on and on,
Crushing,
Reducing each and all
To dust and ash,
To an essence of pain and futile void.
Whether I stay or leave,
I cannot change this.

"In what battle when you rode me did we not prevail?" the noble horse replies. "What enemy have we two not overcome?" Gesar merely turns his head away, lies down and closes his eyes. "It looks like right now you don't want my help," his steed sneers. "Even all the dharma protectors left here some time ago, though you may not have noticed. I think I shall do likewise. Should you need me, call my name. I, for one, shall be playing in brighter, warmer fields." And with that Kyang Ko Kar Kar leaps up and vanishes like a spark in the sky.

*

The Dharma Protector Vajrasadhu Appears

Days pass without change. Gesar often neglects to eat and, daily, he becomes weaker. His mind seems to hover in the air above his body. But one afternoon, a muted roll of thunder draws his attention to the south where a flock of crows are swirling aloft in the gray opalescent skies.

A few days later, he hears the jingle of armor and sees the dark speck of a solitary rider approaching. Now visible against the white sky and snow, now disappearing, the rider picks his way slowly through the swales and drifts. As he draws nearer, Gesar sees a tall, broad-shouldered man, dusty and mud-spattered with a dark red face, eyes pale blue and bloodshot, hair a dirty, reddish gold. He wears a round red leather hat with a broad brim. Beneath his heavy faded crimson cape, he wears black armor streaked with rust. A broadsword with a gilded grip hangs from his waist, and a leopard skin quiver and black bow are strapped to his saddle. He rides on a large white goat with twisted horns. Jauntily, he rides up to Gesar's cave.

"Hah, friend." the stranger booms out boisterously. "Only a sorrowful man, I think, would hide himself in such a place." Gesar, not wanting to engage the man, shrugs, but the stranger will not be deterred. He comes closer and stares at the Lion Lord. "Yes, oh yes, I do know you. You are Gesar, King of Ling."

"I do not recall you." Gesar replies curtly.

"No? Well, I may have seen you from far off. But this is indeed fortunate, here in the middle of nowhere to meet none other than Gesar of Ling." Then the stranger asks if Gesar has seen his attendants and caravan. Somehow he has become separated from them. Gesar shakes his head, even as the stranger describes a great cavalcade of heavy-laden camels and mounted warriors traveling North and Westward with his wives and goods. Gesar remains stonily silent at this dubious tale, but the traveler goes on equably. "Oh well. I'll find them soon."

Then the visitor leaps lightly from his mount, digs into a saddlebag, pulls out a large bottle, and strides towards Gesar. "We must however take a moment and drink to this fortunate coincidence." And with that he sits down next to Gesar, uncorks the bottle and politely hands it to him. "Please... Drink."

Gesar, at a loss for what else to do, drinks. It is a tangy rice wine of a kind Gesar has never tasted before, and he finds it very much to his liking. Soon visitor and guest have passed the bottle back and forth a good number of times and both have drunk a good deal. The visitor asks Gesar about his reasons for sequestering himself in such an obscure place. Gesar is not inclined to answer, but in the end tells his guest all he has seen and heard of his mother, her life and her torments. And he confesses that the cause of his deepest sorrow is his uncertainty about how to save her.

The strange guest shakes his head. "Indeed, great lord, it is true, as is said, that the realms of suffering are notorious for their endlessness. But they also say that the Buddha has liberated beings even from Hell itself. I can show you how he did so. Perhaps this can guide you."

And with that, he reaches into his robe and draws out a scroll. As he holds it aloft in his left hand, it unfurls to reveal a sequence of brightly colored scenes. Then pointing to these illustrations one by one, he recites a story in his bright melodious voice.

"Many years ago, when the Buddha still lived upon this earth, he had a disciple, Maudgalyayana. And this disciple had a vision. He saw his mother in the depths of hell, pinned with red-hot iron nails to a red-hot iron bed. Steel discs flew through the air and cut her flesh and bronze ravens picked at her eyes and heart.

"Distraught, he went to the Buddha and sought his advice. The Awakened One told his disciple first to make offerings to the Three Jewels and in that way Maudgalyayana would arouse the strength to free his mother from the ever shifting states of mind in which she had entrapped herself.

"Maudgalyayana went to hell itself to show the poor woman the causes of her misfortune. He showed how suffering and dissatisfaction were the inescapable nature of all existence and that the hell she inhabited was created by her own rage.

"Hearing this," he continues, "she was liberated into the hungry ghost realm. Maudgalyayana followed her there and showed her how craving produced that world. Thus she ascended to the animal realm. In the animal realm, Maudgalyayana showed his mother the truth of cessation, the end of dreamy ignorance. In the human realm he taught her the way of conduct that avoids the extremes of nihilism and eternalism. In the Asura realm, he taught the meaning of emptiness that cuts through fixation on outer phenomena. Finally in the realm of the gods, he showed her that compassion cuts through self-absorption and lights the way through all the realms.

"As you well know, Great Lord, from moment to moment, our moods alter our world, and the six realms of being arise from our passions. They move within us, and we project them outward as our reality. Thus, passing through all these realms, Maudgalyayana's mother was liberated."

Perhaps it is the stranger's hypnotic way of chanting, or perhaps he is just overcome by the unfamiliar wine, but it seems to Gesar that as the stranger points to each part of the scroll and gives the teachings associated with each realm, it comes alive before his eyes. He feels as if he's seen the Buddha and his disciple walking together in the balmy forest groves of India. He weeps when he sees Maudgalyayana's mother engulfed in Hell. In the Preta realm, he is wracked by hunger and disappointment. In the animal realm it is as if needs and fears press him onward in a dreamy sleep. When the stranger evokes the human realm, Gesar is overcome by thoughts and possibilities, and in the Asura realm by his own furious ambitions. And when the story ends, Gesar suddenly wakes from the vast bliss of the God Realm. He finds himself sitting with this strange storyteller before a cave in the snow. But within his weight of sadness, Gesar begins to feel a glimmer of hope. Then the traveler sings:

Suffering is an endless chain of cause and effect.
Liberation is spontaneous, awake.

Because the awakened state is the natural state,
There is no separation or non-separation.
Because wisdom is spontaneous presence,
There is no obstruction or absence of obstruction.
Because compassion is the natural way of acting,
There is no hesitation and no certainty.

Surrender completely to the world of phenomena:
Love is the gateway and the offering.
This is the light of freedom.

Gesar now sees what he must do to save his mother and he wants to ask for more advice. But suddenly he is too drunk to find the words. The visitor pats him gently on the shoulder.

"Great Lord, even as the sun and moon and stars cross the sky from East to West and do not stop, go in that direction. You must climb the Western Mountains. It is a terrible journey past the edge of the world. As you climb, the four elements of your body will collapse one into the other. You can rely only on your great heart and your unconquerable resolve. Great Hero, I have no doubt you will succeed." Gesar nods and exhausted, keels over.

Gesar then dreams that he is walking North and Westward through the snow, and as he comes over a rise, he encounters a great encampment of lavishly embroidered tents with fine horses tethered all about. He hears music, singing and laughter, and smells smoke and roasting meat.

When he enters the camp he is greeted by his former guest who is now resplendent in clean clothes and polished armor. He is seated at the center of a long table covered in scarlet silk and filled with silver plates of steaming meat and crystal pitchers of many kinds of wine. All around warriors are wrestling, singing, playing dice; women are dancing in circles and practicing divination with mirrors.

"Ah, Great King, welcome," The stranger booms and stretches out his hand indicating a place that has been prepared for the Lion Lord between two of his wives, one dark and buxom and the other fair and slender. Both women feed Gesar, cutting meat from great haunches of venison with their daggers, holding it on the blade's sharp point and putting it into his mouth. They give him drinks from their own goblets and flirt brazenly with him, stroking his legs beneath the table. Gesar blushes and looks up at his host who merely winks.

Sometime later in the night, Gesar finds himself standing arm in arm with his host beside a huge iron cauldron and peering at it. A soup, seemingly vast as a lake, boils madly. Gesar looks into the churning liquid, and sees a body, which suddenly he recognizes as his own.

"Look!" he shouts. "That is my leg. And there, there, that arm, and the head, and look, the chest: they're mine too." And the two laugh wildly as they watch Gesar's dismembered corpse cook in the soup. The stranger suddenly kisses Gesar hard on the lips and bites him, causing a faint taste of blood to fill his mouth.

"All the realms of life and death are very near. You can have whatever you want," he hisses fiercely, and he presses something into Gesar's hand. "Give this to whomever you love."

In the morning when Gesar wakes, there is no sign of his drinking companion. He rolls over and groans with a terrible headache. The encampment has vanished. A strong scent of juniper smoke lingers in the air. On the collar of his shirt, Gesar smells a woman's perfume. As he stretches, he finds a small metal box in his hand,

and in it a small roll of yellow silk with strange writing in red ink. Although he has never before seen such writing, somehow its meaning is plain. Thus he reads:

The Roaring Laughter of the Innate which Deceives and Paralyzes All Self Delusion; an invocation to Vajrasadhu, the Supreme Warrior Protector of the Pure Dharma

Great Vajrasadhu, Illusion King
Lord of the Palace of the Six Realms of Being,
If there is wrath, whatever is known is your domain.
If there is pride, whatever is possessed is your domain.
If there is desire, whatever is sensed is your domain.
If there is envy, whatever is imagined is your domain.

Wherever anything arises based on cause and effect,
Lord of Illusion's Endless Play, you appear.
Your body is spontaneous illusion.
Your speech is spontaneous experience.
Your mind is spontaneous awareness.

You wear the round leather helmet of the samaya-bound
Surmounted by the golden wish-fulfilling gem.
Your face is dark red and your three bloodshot eyes flash wildly.
Your hair, eyebrows and beard are golden flames.
Your gold and ruby earrings jangle
As you dance in all the bardo states.

With tongue curled back, you snarl and laugh,
Shouting the sounds of HAH and HO and HEE.
Doubt, self-deception and guile are your food,
Lies, schemes and seduction your favorite drinks.
The entire range of illusion is your plate and goblet.

The swirls of your vast crimson cape
Are the confusion of the six realms.
Your armor is made from conceptual thinking.
Duplicity, conceit and hidden lust
Are the silver ribbons adorning your helmet and sleeves.
Because you do not hesitate to put your hand into any madness
You hold in your right hand a nine-pointed golden dorje.

Because you completely consume all illusion, leaving nothing behind,
You hold a pulsing human heart in your left hand.

Emerging suddenly from your vast Southern palace,
You ride on a turquoise he-goat with twined coral horns
Who emits the pungent scent of every possibility, delightful and repulsive.
You enter this world sometimes slowly, sometimes suddenly,
Sometimes larger than a giant mountain,
Sometimes smaller than a house-fly.

You are surrounded by your retinue
Of one hundred voluptuous and flirtatious dakinis,
Singing, dancing and telling fortunes.
One hundred powerful warriors--
Boastful, lascivious, clever in strategy and oblique attack--
Are your bodyguards.

Chief of your retinue, and arrayed like you,
Carrying golden hammer and bellows,
Is the great artificer, maker of all manner of weapons,
Jewelry, tools, illusions and ingenious diversions.

Your caravan fills the sky like billowing smoke,
And the air is filled with a deafening roar
Of laughter, sobs, chatter, jokes, screams, curses, and whispers.
Monkeys and bears augment the maddening din.

Oh Great Vajrasadhu, you are the supreme protector
Of the dharma that is all pervasive in and beyond form,
The dharma that cannot be limited or circumscribed,
That is beyond truth or falsehood, piety or impiety
Beyond practice or attainment.

You alone protect the purity of the dharma.
You alone protect the reality of the dharma.
You alone protect the life of the dharma.
You alone protect the spontaneity of the dharma.
You alone protect the shocking wonder of the dharma.

Now in this time, when the materialistic outlook
Infests every mind, and all act with an eye to self-advantage;
When logics and fake knowledge are common currency;
The dharma has become an artifact to be bartered.

The Hinayana dharma has become a pretext for fearful rigidity;
The Mahayana has become a pretext for stylishness and condescension;
The sublime Vajrayana has become a pretext
For sloppiness, fraud, and cosmic self-aggrandizement.

Now those who claim to be inspired
Are merely wild and unstable.
Those who claim to be devoted
Are merely desperate and dogmatic;
Those who claim to be of an independent mind
Are merely fickle and self-absorbed;
And those who claim to be ordinary
Are merely resentful and intentionally ignorant.
This time now calls out to you.

Now, Now, Now Vajrasadhu, enter this world
With your carnival of Dharma Protectors,
Shake, turn, wheel, dance, eat, laugh and sing.
Please, as your feast offering,
Consume the mountain of our self-deceived seriousness
And the blood oceans of our self-serving depression and excitement.
Let the true dharma explode in every noise,
Every desire, every color, every taste, every now.

Supreme protector, be with us in this instant.
Be our awake
And do not depart.
HOH HEE HOH HOH HEE HAH
SARVA DHARMA MANGALA SVAHA

After reading this, Gesar, Lion King of Ling falls back into unconsciousness. When
he wakes, he sets out resolutely in the direction that his remarkable host has suggested.

*

Collapse of the Four Great Elements

Gesar travels for five days and nights. His journey becomes ever more arduous as he climbs upward through the Western mountains. Sometimes he feels as if he is completely insane ever to have set out on this quest; other times it feels completely right.

On the first day, the path is easy, passing over hard-packed snow through rolling pastures and fields. But as he progresses, the snow becomes softer and deeper. Gesar feels his body becoming heavier and heavier, sinking down into the snow. Memories of being buried assail him. It is as if once again he is in the pit where his uncle Todong had buried him or again in the hole where he concealed himself from Lutzen, Demon Lord of the North. He cannot tell if he is making any headway or simply churning in his own claustrophobia.

As night falls and he walks on, it seems like he is sinking down into the soil. The smell of moldering leaves and rotting corpses engulf him. Nothing is real except the damp crushing pressure all around. He begins to hallucinate. He sees in vague outline the tunnels of foxholes bending through the shadows around him. He is surrounded by mice and woodchucks asleep in their burrows, centipedes crawling through tunnels, ground hornets stirring in their nests, huge cities of teeming ants. Gesar feels that a great serpent is coiled about him, and his mind becomes strangely sluggish. All his tangible and logical experiences are collapsing. He forces himself to shout:

"Whatever in this body is made of earth,
Let it return to earth as offering to the Three Jewels,
The essence, nature, and display of empty space.
May all that is solid in my body nourish all beings
And ease the pains of death."

Repeating this, he presses on, as if driven by a tremor pulsing through a darkness dense with shadows.

The next day, Gesar is less oppressed. The path is steeper and leads upward through dank forests of pine and juniper. He hears a distant waterfall, and as he climbs higher, its roar becomes greater and greater, drowning out every other sound. The trees become shorter and more stunted, wreathed in dense drifting mist. He continues onward, and the thundering sound is so great that Gesar can hear nothing else. Looming out of the thick fog, twisted trees take the form of writhing ghosts whose cries of longing are lost in the din of falling water. Gesar pushes himself to climb faster. He wants to speed onward as he had in the horse race when he won his right to rule Ling. His skin and clothes are now soaked. He feels mist filling his lungs. It is becoming impossible to breathe and he is drowning amid the tumultuous sound of cascading water. Tears run down his cheeks as deep waves of emotion rise and shake him. He shouts:

"Let whatever in this body is water,
Dissolve into water as offering to the Three Jewels,
The essence, nature and compassion of empty space.
May all that is liquid in my body slake the thirst of all beings
And ease the pains of birth."

And repeating this, as if driven by a tidal wave, Gesar presses on.

On the third day, Gesar enters a shimmering canyon of ice and rock carved by a glacial stream into the mountains' granite flanks. He clambers over slippery boulders, clings to sharp promontories, crawls along narrow broken ledges as he makes his ascent. The moisture on his face, hands and clothing freeze. He feels that even his flesh is freezing and cracking. All heat is leaving his body.

In this landscape of rock and ice, there is no life at all, and there is no scent of anything. As the sun sets, the rocks assume the shape of giant demons with mocking tortured faces. Sometimes these images are clear and other times hazy. Gesar can no longer remember why he has undertaken this journey. Memories of his love for Sechan Dugmo and his hatred of the Lord of Hor who abducted her, of his passionate sojourn with Lutzen's wife, of his destruction of King Shingti; these and many other moments flicker and dissolve before him. His field of vision is filled with sparks flying all around, as if he were himself a bonfire giving out its last heat in the dark. He cries:

"Let the heat of this body be consumed in its own nature
As offering to the Three Jewels,
The essence, nature and display of empty space.
May all the warmth in my body give comfort to all beings
And ease the pains of sickness."

And rousing himself to fight an implacable foe, Gesar, as if running from a forest fire, races on.

On the next day, Gesar emerges on a vast high snow-field. The snow is frozen solid like a silver mirror, and the air is cold and thin. But the path is level, and the Lion Lord, moves across this unchanging landscape with no feeling of effort. Slowly he loses all sense of his body, but breathing becomes ever more labored in the empty air.

Gasping for breath as he trudges on, his sense of even being human begins to dissolve. It is as if he is losing himself in certain moments he experienced during spiritual practice on solitary retreat. The world flickers before his eyes like a lamp going out. He feels bewildered and somehow insubstantial, as visions of celestial deities and great warriors flash around him.

"So let air return to itself
As offering to the Three Jewels,
The essence, nature and compassion of empty space.
May all the breath in my body give life to all other beings
And ease the pains of old age."

Gesar cries out over and over. He pushes forward even as he feels he is nothing more than a leaf in a gale.

On the morning of the fifth day, Gesar climbs to a small summit from which he sees a serried range of snow mountains looming, rank on rank before him. He is exhausted and feverish. A sharp pain burns at the top of his head, and although it is only morning, he spreads his robes on the snow and collapses.

The white light of a frozen sun pervades the white snow fields and the bright pearly sky. As Gesar lies there, the entire world and his thoughts and memories of it dissolve slowly into a bright milky mist. All anger, and all kinds of lesser irritations dissolve into this whiteness and peace. As the mind of anger dissolves, the world of discrete phenomena collapses.

In the afternoon, the sun turns scarlet and fills the sky. Gesar seems to faint. The air, the sky, the earth are all nothing but bright all-pervasive red light. All thoughts of desire and longing are embraced and absorbed in fire light. As the mind of passion consumes itself, all sense of time melts.

At night, the Lion Lord's world and mind are plunged into complete and utter blackness. He can no longer tell if he is experiencing something or not, or even if he still exists. As the mind of ignorance ends, all sense of space comes to an end.

Early next morning, Gesar finds himself facing directly into the rising sun whose blazing light fills all the earth and sky and whole of space. There is no center and no edge. This light is awareness itself; there is no knower or perceiver or thing to be known or perceived. There is panic and the urge to pull away. Even this thought becomes nothing more than an instant of light.

He sleeps, and then begins to dream. He dreams of his birth, his childhood, his deeds; he dreams of his teachers, his companions, his consorts, his kingdom, his world, his visions and his journeys. His heart is filled with sadness and love.

At noon, when Gesar wakes, it is as if he has just lived through his whole life in a dream. Still dazed, he puts on his robe, lights a fire of juniper. He feels he can travel no further on his own, and so he calls out for the miracle horse Kyang Ko Kar Kar.

"Hoh, little horse, best friend and wind of life, come to me now from wherever you graze in the starry expanse of space." Then he lies downs and gazes at the summit of the sky.

A small turquoise dot appears in the center of the sky; it becomes a line, then a curve, then a two dimensional shadow. Then suddenly like a silver javelin, the miracle horse descends from the air. His dark bay coat gleams, the tips of his ears are like pennants, his black mane swirls, and his long black tail flies like smoke behind him. His harness is adorned with gold and silver, his saddle adorned with coral and turquoise; his stirrups are copper colored gold and his saddle blanket is of snow leopard. As his onyx hooves strike the ground before Gesar, sparks explode all around him.

The wonder horse, Kyang Ko Kar Kar had been grazing on the vast expanses of the steppe when he heard the faint echo of Gesar's call. In a single bound, he has come instantly to Gesar's side. But the miracle steed does not find Gesar dressed, full of energy, prepared to act. Gesar is lying listlessly on the rocky floor before the same cave where Kyang Ko Kar Kar left him.

Kyang Ko Kar Kar nuzzles Gesar's chest, but he senses only the faintest rise and fall of breath within the body of the Lion Lord. Gesar lies on the ground like an effigy of sand. Kyang Ko Kar Kar presses his nose against Gesar's pale hand. It is almost cold; his grayish cheek is barely warm.

After the many battles they have fought together and the many dangers they have overcome, the Horse of Wind cannot imagine anything in the three realms capable of bringing King Gesar to this state. But he does know that somewhere within King Gesar, the fire of life still burns. It is impossible that it not be so. Carefully then, Kyang Ko Kar Kar hoists Gesar up onto his jade saddle, rises slowly up into the air, and carries the unconscious body of the King of Ling back to his homeland.

Amid the purple clouds and turquoise mists of the afternoon sky, bolts of lightning and squalls of freezing rain tear through the air all about the winged horse and his stricken rider. From afar, it sounds as if the air itself is keening and screaming with rage.

As she sits outside her black tent with its pennants and banners, Sechan Dugmo, Gesar's wife and Queen of Ling hears these terrible sounds and her heart fills with apprehension. She looks into the sky where the storm rages, and although Kyang Ko Kar Kar and his master look no larger than a pebble tossed in the air, she somehow knows what she will see. And when they come closer, and she sees Gesar's body lying across the noble horse's back, a great cry rips from her throat.

Others, shocked by her cry, look. Soon wails and shouts of dismay fill the air. Everyone runs toward Gesar's tent. So when Kyang Ko Kar Kar lands on the ground, he is met by Gesar's weeping wife and family, solemn rows of ministers and generals, crowds of sobbing warriors and citizens.

As the miracle horse walks slowly towards the queen, there is only silence. No one can imagine Gesar wounded or dying, and none has ever considered the possibility of a life without his presence. All are stunned as inwardly each looks at a future that looms ahead like a sudden precipice. Then in a deep and sonorous voice, the miracle horse speaks:

"Great Queen, Noble Lords, Warriors of Ling. I have traveled far to return now with the King of Ling. We reached a cave in the desert and he stopped. He sat there for a long time in silence. Then he sent me away. You all saw his mood before he left here. It had only worsened. But on the instant of his call, I flew to him and found him as you see."

The people of Ling now stare at the pale inert form that lies across the saddle on Kyang Ko Kar Kar's back. Suddenly fear grips them all as they find themselves lost on a frozen empty plane. Fear fills their hearts: fear for the kingdom, fear for their own safety and for that of their families. Their future dreams are suddenly stripped away.

Then, almost inaudibly, Sechan Dugmo asks the Horse of Wind: "How is it that this Great Lord who feared nothing in the world and whom no enemy, whether God, Human, or Naga could defeat, now is broken so?" And she gestures at Gesar who looks almost like a corpse.

"No enemy could do this," Kyang Ko Kar Kar replies. "Only Gesar himself has such power, and only something within him brings him to this state. He is at the very gate of death and does not breathe, but the warmth of life has not departed. Whether he will now live or not, I cannot say, but you must tend to him. Make him warm and comfortable. Keep him close within your heart."

As Gesar's generals lift their leader's body off the horse's back, the crowd's fear boils into a rage at whatever could conceivably have caused such a disaster. Someone from the back of the crowd throws a stone at Kyang Ko Kar Kar. It hits him on his hind quarters where it shatters into a cloud of dust. Some snicker, others nod approvingly.

In a fury, the Wind Horse shoots up into the air in a tornado of sparks. Baring his long teeth, he whirls and emits a neigh which shakes the tents of the people of Ling.

I have lived at the summit in the sky
And I am the wind that moves with time.

I am the quickness of the awakened mind,
And the lord of goodness rides on my sleek back.

Carrying the great hero of compassion, Gesar of Ling,
I have flown through countless realms of bliss and terror.

From low to high, great to small,
I have assumed a thousand shapes.
In myriad guises I have raged in battle,
Languished in sulfurous dungeons,
Held myself inert as stone,
Outsped every other creature of the earth and sky.

I am wind and swift movement
Yet I have never seen such fickleness as I see now.
I am accustomed to appearing in many forms
But I have never seen beings change themselves so carelessly.

You imagine that this great King
Who has been the light of your lives is dead.
So your minds turn to your own survival,
And you seek to hide in darkness like animals.

You believe that this Great Warrior,
Who has seen to the nourishment and well being of your world,
Has no more power
And suddenly, you are starving like Hungry Ghosts.

You think that this Great Lord
Who has conquered every inner and outer enemy
Has abandoned you,
And you cower and rave like beings in Hell.

I am movement itself,
But I do not waver.
I am a constellation of forms
But my nature does not change.

I am inseparable from Gesar, Lion Lord of Ling.
And as we pass from life to life and death to death,
Every obstacle and hardship
Protects us from the drifting dreams of sleep.

From awake to awake,
Our journey together does not end.

And with that, the Horse of Wind disappears into an empty sky like a flash of light.

Chastened and abashed, the people of Ling stand in silence as Gesar's body is carried into his tent and placed beneath silk sheets and bearskins. Sechan Dugmo tends him day and night, pouring drops of broth between his ashen lips, bathing him, holding him dear in heart and mind while the people of Ling wait.

Far off on the high snow covered alpine tundra where the whole world seems made of stars and thin sparkling snow, Odkar Gyaltsan, son of Gesar's half brother and

Gesar's appointed heir, sleeps in his tent. As Gesar had asked him, he has been on retreat for some months, and the time has passed easily. But that night, he has a frightening dream. He sees Gesar's corpse sitting on a throne in a dark tent, wreathed in clouds of incense. He hears the sound of women weeping and men crying. At this unearthly wail, Odkar Gyaltsan wakes suddenly, and out of an unaccountable fear and longing, sings this song.

Great Father Gesar,
Only you show the true path that is reality itself.
You are anointed in power
By the sheer reality of your being.

I, your heir,
Am chosen by you
But am not you.
I am not your equal.

No practice, act, insight or knowledge
Can change this.

Please do not abandon me.
Please bless your unworthy son,
That the joy of the living path of wakefulness
Shine out in the life of every instant.

Please do not leave my heart.
Bless me, your future king,
That a vision of enlightened society
Will radiate forever in the heart of all.

*

Encountering Vetali: The Great Zero Point
Here it is told how Gesar meets the great Vetali, who is the zero point at the juncture of life and death. He hears the song called: The Black Mirror of Vajra Space. This song is accompanied by offerings and music.

But as far as Gesar himself is concerned, he continues on his journey. Overjoyed at seeing Kyang Ko Kar Kar once again, Gesar touches his head to that of the noble steed. He buckles on his crystal sword, tightens his golden armor, puts on his crystal helmet with its four white silk pennants, and swings up into the saddle of the prancing stallion. As one, they leap up and up, directly through the burning sun in the center of the noon sky, and shoot into the heart of empty space.

Gesar, Lion Lord of Ling astride the tireless Horse of Wind, Kyang Ko Kar Kar flies through an endless shining expanse of space and light.

No wind or air touches them, and there is no outer variation of any kind. There is no dawn or noon or dusk. There are no clouds or mist, no mountain peaks, no distant vistas. No up. No down. Thus, even though they move, there is no time.

Careening joyfully through the trackless white expanse of space, horse and rider wonder if this journey could ever end. At that moment, in the Northern sky appears a minute black raging cloud and they turn to move toward it.

There, emerging from the non-dual point before the division of space and phenomena, comes a song without sound and a vision without words. Whether Gesar hears or sings it, he does not know. The song is called The Black Mirror of Vajra Space.

AH BHYO HUM
Arising in the luminous emptiness of primordial space,
As dot,
As roar,
As great storm cloud,
As flame,
As drum beat,
As terror,
As bliss,

Now as deity,
Great Vetali, indifferent to every outcome,
You give and at that same instant consume
The life of all life.

AH
Non-duality is duality.
BHYO
This is the reunion of mother and child.

Only those consumed by the heart of compassion
Can know you.
Only those completely moved by love
Can see you:
The one being who is the beginning and the end

HUM
Surrounded by twisting clouds of oily black smoke
Which fill the whole of space,
Lit from within by raging walls of thick, red volcanic flame,
Shooting sparks of exploding suns, moons on fire,
Galaxies being ripped apart,
Seated on a throne of fire,
Your terrifying face and vast sinuous body
Shine like a polished obsidian sky.

All joyful,
Your hair and eyebrows are burning fire.
Origin of time,
You have three eyes, filled with boiling blood.
Primordial luminous omniscience,
From your every glance
Shoot world-consuming lightning bolts of rage.

All consuming great bliss,
Your steel fangs gnash with the sound of thunder.
Saliva and blood glisten on your grinning lips.
Exhausting all wisdom,
You wear a crown of five dried skulls.

Origin of all life,
The wish-fulfilling jewel glows in your hair.
Origin of all action,
You have four arms,
And with your every movement
Worlds rise, flourish, burn and are dispersed,
As your gestures tear through the shining heart of space.

In your raised right hand
You swing a double-edged sword of meteoric iron,
Cutting through everything,
Revealing everything.

In your raised left hand,
You hold a long-life arrow
Which pierces the root of the universal unconscious.

It is adorned with Garuda's feathers.
Its shaft, made from the axle tree of all existence,
Runs through a living human head.

Its point, also of meteoric iron,
Is adorned with furls of bloody spray.
Amid this spray a golden mirror, bright as the sun
Which reflects all the forms of life and time.

In your lower right hand
You hold a skull cup as large as the cosmos
Filled with boiling blood.
In its center is Mount Meru adorned with the six realms.

In your lower left hand is a phurba
Made from the primordial razor knife
Which pierces the life of every passion.

Because your being is unimagined, unseen,
And utterly without thought, you are naked.
Because you sever the root of endless ignorance,
You wear the freshly flayed hide of a white elephant.
And because life and death are trivial adornments,
You wear a necklace of human bone.

As if riding on the sky itself,
You ride on a donkey, pale as a corpse
With a white blaze like a noon day sun

Your form is so immense
That none can see it all at once.

The noise surrounding you is deafening,
Both shrill and deep
As if the sky and everything beneath it
Is being shredded and crushed,
And all the oceans, rivers, lakes and seas sucked dry.

Your expression is seductive, cruel, and indifferent
Languidly, you offer a skull cup

Filled with a sea of blood
And torma of the six realms at its center.

This torma is Mount Meru itself.
Near its summit are luminous palaces and iridescent parks.
These are the abode of the gods and goddesses
Who dwell in formless and formed realms.

Below them, on the flanks and ravines of the world-axis Mountain,
Are the great cities of the Asuras
With their protective walls of gold, silver, bronze and iron.

Lower still are the societies of the human realm,
And below and amidst them, the world of the animals
Running in herds, schools, families, and hiding in solitude.

Pervading these latter two places
Is the domain of the hungry ghosts, haunted and desolate.
Then below them all, extending to unimaginable depths
Are the many realms of boiling and freezing hells.

All the realms are filled with innumerable beings:
Resting, sated, delirious, plotting,
Struggling, running, yearning, dying.
The noises emerging from this panoply of life
Stun all the senses.

From the torma mountain of life rise terrible odors
Of feces and rot, dust and mold, sweat, and forged metal.
From here also the most refined and delicious scents waft through the air.
Thought is overwhelmed and paralyzed.

Vetali, Vetali, Life of Life
Beyond thought, beyond reason, beyond preference,
Beyond desire, beyond longing, beyond meaning,
You are reality.

With smacking lips like the sounds of love,
You sound the end of consciousness,
You consume all that makes up life, appearance, deception, and purpose.
You devour the fantasies of liberation.

All that makes up life, appearance, deception, and purpose
Is the rich and delicious food that sustains you.
You devour liberation itself.

Accept us as your offering:
We who are inspired by the guru's single word,
We who uphold our vows,
We who are fickle,
We whose minds wander,
We who are sincere frauds or simply criminals.
In the purity of dharmata,
Please accept us.

Keep the reality that cannot be overcome,
The reality that cannot be owned, evaded or manipulated,
The reality that cannot be mastered
Ever before us.

Keep us in the mirror of your being,
O, Supreme Vetali of the three realms.
Hold us in the burning heart of life
A LI LI

The great demoness smiles, showing her double row of glittering razor fangs. Vetali then extends the enormous boiling kapala of blood with its torma in the shape of Mount Meru and the six realms to the great hero and his steed, and in her hypnotic and inescapable silence command: "Accept this."

Gesar yanks Kyang Ko Kar Kar's reins and the miraculous steed rears up. They leap across the great steaming ocean of blood in the skull cup towards the towering torma of Mount Meru.

Even as they begin to rise through the scalding steam, rider and mount smell the bloody breath of the demoness. They hear the thunderous crash of steel teeth coming together around them, and are engulfed in darkness.

*

PART 2
PASSAGES IN THE REALMS OF LIFE AND DEATH

The Kingdom of Yama, Lord of Death
Gesar's love for the one who gave him birth, the Naga Princess Dzeden, and his great heart for the sufferings of all beings draw him on. Steadfast in his resolve to enter the natural liberation of the bardos and realms, he passes into the kingdom of Yama, the Lord of Death. To the accompaniment of heavy drumbeats, crashing cymbals, and low horns, this is chanted in a deep voice.

Gesar, Lord of Warriors and his horse of wind, Kyang Ko Kar Kar drop like a meteor through a lightless sky, descending through swirling clouds of thickening black smoke. The heat around them becomes ever greater. Gesar's armor begins to burn against his skin, and his clothes begin to scorch. Suddenly there is a great crash as if an iron gate has just swung closed behind them. At the same instant, the steel hooves of the horse of miracles strike a great polished iron floor with the metallic clash of swords striking armor.

The air ripples with sheets of flame and spumes of black burning smog, and reeks of sweat, blood, and burning flesh. Seething vapors scald their throats and lungs, and they almost cannot breathe. Blinded, Ko Kar Kar rears in panic. Gesar cries out and gropes desperately for his sword.

A deafening metallic roar of thunder rolls through the dense air. Gesar feels he is in the center of an immense bronze bell, and the pulsing sound waves are shaking the atoms in his body apart.

Then a wild cacophony of screams, wails, piercing shrieks, and mocking laughter erupts all around. Kyang Ko Kar Kar wheels madly as Gesar searches desperately through the dark choking air. Slowly, as they twist and turn, their eyes, still stinging from the heat and fumes, become accustomed to the reeking darkness. They see they are in an immense white-hot iron prison house so vast that they can find neither its walls nor its ceiling. Its ancient rusting steel walls are banked with heaps of glowing coals. It is as if they are surrounded by a ring of bonfires circling the horizon of a sunless earth.

As fuming smoke whirls around their faces, it takes on the flickering shapes of a myriad of demons who brush against them leaving slimy traces of spit and mucus. Black demons with crows' heads, human bodies and iron wings fly past, carrying naked writhing corpses in their iron beaks. Phosphorescent green owls with the faces of old women and talons of bronze hoot as they rip brains out of skulls. Vultures red as embers with bloody claws at the end of their muscular human arms pull the entrails from screaming people not yet dead. Beneath them, smoke-colored jackals race across the iron floor carrying bits of flesh in their grinning mouths, while copper-colored serpents with bland pale human faces undulate, twisting and crushing the bodies of children and women in their coils.

Here and there in the shadows, crowds of naked men, women, children, some weak and bony, others in their prime, huddle together. They cower in helpless terror as they wait for a fate they can neither comprehend nor escape.

Kyang Ko Kar Kar's mouth is foaming and his great body shakes uncontrollably. The chaos of horrific sounds, smells and sights pressing in around him make Gesar think he himself will go mad. Paralyzed for perhaps for a moment or perhaps a century, he sees that at the center of this burning prison is a towering, red-hot iron throne resting on a mountainous pyre of burning corpses.

This is the throne of the Lord of Death, and standing before it, seeming at first like the shadow of an eclipse, then appearing in his full form, is Yama, King of Finality.

Yama towers black and immense with powerful gleaming arms and legs like world-ending monsoons of fire and oily smoke. His huge black body throbs, radiating intense heat but covered in beads of ice-cold corpse-sweat. With flashes of lightning, his steel mesh robe swirls around him, but does not conceal his erection with its burning red tip. He wears an iron belt from which hang hundreds of freshly severed heads of men young and old, beautiful women, crones, adolescents, and infants.

At the top of his neck, which is like a great twisting column of smoke, his bull's head glows like molten bronze. Burning air and sulfurous smoke pour from his nostrils, his ears, and from around his three eyes and ears. Molten lava oozes from his nostrils. His great horns are steel and freezing cold. He wears a crown of dried skulls. His mane blazes wildly like an all-consuming fire. His three eyes, red with burning blood, roll madly scouring the whole of space. Fresh blood stains his smacking lips and gnashing steel teeth. In his right hand he brandishes a huge iron mace surmounted by a huge laughing skull. In his left hand, he holds coils of iron chains with razor hooks.

The Lord of Death stands on a great red bull that is copulating with a beautiful dark-haired giantess. As the King of Death's obsidian toenails rake the bull's back, it bucks and bellows, tearing into the flesh of the giantess below. But she, insensible to the mutilation of her body, writhes and moans in delirium.

Gesar is completely overwhelmed by the totality of this hallucination. Wherever he looks, he is consumed by the phantasmagoria of death, and now in whatever direction he turns his head, the Lord of Death, wild and all consuming, rages before him. There is no direction where the figure of death can be evaded.

Then the Lord of Death himself speaks in an excruciating voice of bronze:

I am the iron gate that closes time:
Lord of the branding iron.

I am the cauldron of cause and effect:
Lord of transformation.

I am the mirror of your hidden face:
Lord of burning chains.

Who you were once
Is no more.

Who you are to be
You will not know.

As the roar of the Lord of Death shakes him, Gesar feels crushed as if all his powers and attainments, his successes and failures, his pride and valor, his cleverness, his wisdom, his realization had become the jaws of a vise closing on him. He knows that all his past cannot sustain him now.

He feels he has pompously proclaimed his story-book role as hero and savior. Now, in his utter helplessness, everything is stripped away. He is completely naked. There is a moment of paralyzing terror: he gives himself up. And suddenly, he feels completely free.

Beyond fear, Gesar draws himself up. His golden armor blazes like the sun and his crystal helmet radiates the cool pervasive light of the full moon. His sword in its scabbard vibrates, and his bow and arrows give off a penetrating hum. Then he sings in a voice clear and strong:

Dying endlessly into every moment,
I am Gesar, Lord of Warriors.
Accepting the embrace of the life
I am the living heart samaya.
Born spontaneously in the luminous empty expanse
I am the ever-youthful vase body.

Then Gesar proclaims: "Neither time nor inescapable fate has brought me here. Willingly, I come before you. My mother, to whom I owe my life and many other kindnesses, is caught within the bonds of Hell. I have come to free her. She suffers horribly. It is my vow to bring her peace, and I will not be stopped."

"Great Hero," and though the Lord of Death attempts to modulate his roaring voice, it is still a loud rasp, "I have heard of you. It is not my doing, noble lord, that your mother suffers so.

"All beings come before me because their life is exhausted. They rise or sink within the six realms because of the weight of their own deeds, words and habitual thoughts. This is the law of existence itself. Everything has its consequence. The judgment of karma and its punishments are inflicted by each being on her or himself.

"Unable to bear the truth of their own responsibility, all the beings of the six realms project my terrible form, my prestige and power."

"My lord," Gesar replies," Your immortality exceeds that of any god. Your voice outlasts the span of any law. Cause and effect spin within your iron grasp. Even the Buddhas must appear subject to your law.

"Every being in every realm fears the approach of the Lord of Death, and even the wisest, most learned, and accomplished beings fear that moment when they will stand before you. Then in your mirror all faults are revealed and all virtues made known. And when they are weighed out, it is you and your servants who carry each being to the realm that reflects the habits of mind which he or she has cultivated. And from those realms you will remove them when the time has come for them to journey on. Thus I request that you conduct me to Hell and find my mother there. Then I will remove her and place her in the human realm once more."

"Peerless Warrior, I do not have the power to free your mother from the endless cycles of existence or from any realm. She alone can free herself. But I will let you show her the entirety of my domain.

"Seeing this, her mind may change. If she can find liberation within the realms and within the flow of life and death, so be it. If not, she returns to her torment."

Gesar smiles: "Thank you, O King. I wish for nothing more except the small favor of your company as a guide." King Yama stared balefully at Gesar. Finally he says:

"Gesar, King of Ling, I do not hold the realms as a possession or a place of which I am merely the lord.

"The six realms are within my body. The nidanas are my veins. The three poisons are my heart's blood. Cause and effect are my heartbeat, and cyclic existence is my breath.

"I am myself the domain of life and death. Thus, wherever you travel in space and time, I am always there. The atoms of all phenomena are the atoms of my being. I pervade all of time and space. The entire expanse of apparent phenomena is my body.

"Choose how you wish to enter: through my mouth, my nose, my ear or my eye, you are welcome."

"If this is a trick, we will be destroyed," whispers Kyang Ko Kar Kar.

Gesar ignores the horse of miracles, and replies simply: "Thank you my lord. We will enter by your center eye."

The Lord of Karma nods his fearsome bull head. "Truly the power of your vow has made you fearless." And by way of a reply, Gesar sings this song in a sweet and gentle voice:

Because of a child's cry and a mother's anxious smile,
My love is Vajra love.
Because of laughter in the snow,
My love is Vajra love.
Because of barley roasting on a pine fire,
My love is Vajra love.
Because of how a horse's whinny carries on a spring breeze,
My love is Vajra love.
Because of a mother's caress by the fireside,
My love is vajra love.
Because of drinking water from a glacier stream,
My love is Vajra love.
Because women laugh as they cut fresh hay,
My love is Vajra love.
Because lovers' tongues meet when they kiss,
My love is vajra love.
Because men boast as they shoot arrows,
My love is Vajra love.
Because old scholars pour over texts in the dim fire light,
My love is Vajra love.
Because every movement is lost beyond recovery,
My love is vajra love.

O lord of Karma,
You are the ax blade
Which brings the endless strands of cause and effect
To the heart of nowness.

As your subject, I die.
My world and my past die.

O Lord of Existence,
You are Mount Meru
On which all the realms of being are arrayed.

Forever
I enter your kingdom with the samaya heart of Vajra love.
I die into nowness.

With that Gesar rises in the saddle on the horse of wind. The two suddenly shrink
to the size of a gnat. They rise through the steaming air that envelopes the Lord of
Death's body. They fly up along his long nose where the sounds of his breathing are
louder than the beating of a hundred watchtower drums. They approach his huge
bloodshot eye which seems as vast a stormy sky, and they enter the opening at its right
corner which looms before them as great tunnel lined with molten lava.

*

Uncertainties in Ling

Gesar's sojourn with the Lord of Death may have lasted less than an hour, but in
Ling, his stricken body lies on the border of life and death for seven days. Sechan
Dugmo keeps him alive by dripping broth through his pale lips. She washes and
massages him and keeps him warm. She sits by him day and night and sings softly
to him.

Where are you now, my sleeping lord?
Where do you venture in shadow and in dream?

Please do not forget that we, your people,
Are tramping in the dark like panicky horses.

Please do not forget me, my warrior king:
Proud and inconstant though I may be,
My heart is bound by love to you.

Please think of us and wake:
Return to us from realms we do not know.
Return and smile on us,
And let us hold you once again.

O where are you now, my sleeping lord?
Where do you venture in shadow and in dream?

From the length and breadth of the kingdom, the great nobles and generals of Ling who have spent their lives in service to the Lion Lord converge and, in a solemn cavalcade, enter the great encampment surrounding Gesar's tent.

Odkar Gyaltsan rides in first on his horse the color of autumn frost. He is the son of Gesar's half brother, Gyatsa Shalkar and the designated heir of the throne of Ling. Youthful and slender, his face is the color of dawn and his expression anxious and inquiring. He wears a robe of red brocade, his armor is reddish gold and his gold helmet is marked with a garuda flying across a full moon.

The great general, second in command of Gesar's armies, Chopa Tongdan rides in on his black charger. Though no longer young, his body is still powerful, and his face is dark with suppressed anger. Having fought for Gesar in many battles, his face and body bear many scars. He wears black leather and a breastplate made of iron. His helmet is marked with an attacking lion.

The married lama and steward of King Gesar's teachings, Norbu Chopel arrives on a blue mare and wears the white robes of a nakpa. He is tall, very thin, and old with white hair and a wispy beard. His face is lined and his expression is peaceful and sad. He wears a cap marked with a silver tiger poised to leap.

The Prime Minister, Tsashang Denma, radiating unswerving confidence, rides in on an immense golden stallion. Though he too is old, his wiry body remains strong and flexible. His hair and beard are still black as onyx. The expression on his broad golden face is unreadable. He wears a golden helmet marked with an obsidian dragon.

These and many other lords and ministers come with their wives, children, attendants and retinues of warriors. Their black tents, each with its own fluttering standards, swell Gesar's encampment and fill all the lowlands. Every day brings more warriors and nobles from distant lands.

Among them is Dikchen Shenpa, Prince of Hor, whom Gesar had made ruler of his former enemy's domain. He arrives on a roan mountain pony. His face is red and puffy and his black eyes dart everywhere as if he were starving. He has a fat belly and long skinny arms and legs. He is dressed in an ostentatious robe of red and gold and he smokes a golden pipe. He has fought for Gesar on many occasions but his manner is shifty.

With him comes Yula Tangyur, Prince of Jang, another who ruled a country Gesar conquered. He rides a large shambling yellow horse, and though he is strong and well proportioned, his expression is timid and furtive. He seems uncomfortable on his own and clings to the company of the Prince of Hor.

The nobles, elders and senior warriors of Ling then meet together in council. All speak of their concern for the future. Some worry that enemies may take advantage of Gesar's illness and attack. Others worry about the morale and discipline of the warriors and subjects. No one dares to discuss the possibility that Gesar could die, but it is in the minds of everyone. Fear permeates all their discussions.

Tsashang Denma, Prime Minister of Ling and long Gesar's main advisor, listens silently. But when the meeting is about to adjourn without having reached any conclusions, he requests permission to sing a song to the people assembled nearby. Turning to the anxious populace of Ling, in a deep and melodious voice he sings:

Gesar, The Celestially Appointed Lion Lord of Ling
Is the golden thread
Which has bound our lives and hearts together.

If this thread should break,
Shall we remain as one,
Or shall we scatter through the ten directions of the earth?

And if we go on separate pathways,
Will this be good or bad?

Our lives, bound together by the golden thread
Of the deeds and battles of the Lion Lord,
Have been extraordinary and heroic.

Will our lives soon become ordinary?
On our own, shall we be subject to long depression,
Selfish lusts, doubt, and petty concerns?

I have met with the Ministers and Elders of Ling,
All of whom enjoy the great Lord's trust.

Warriors insist we must keep up our martial disciplines;
Priests say we must not let our spiritual practice wane;
The mothers and grandmothers say
The raising of the children must not falter;

Herdsmen need to look to their flocks;
Farmers say planting, cultivation and harvest cannot stop;
Artisans insist that the quality of work must be maintained;
Traders need to continue in their work.

All say these things and more
Are essential to the way King Gesar rules in Ling.
And this is true.

But at this moment,
We are poised together with our great king.

Suddenly we find ourselves in a kingdom we did not foresee,
Facing a time we cannot quite understand.

Now, just as when we were attacked by the Horpa
Or fought against the great warriors of King Shingti
And the hordes of Jang,
Now, as then,
The golden light of the Lion Lord's vast being
Must not wane or flicker in our hearts.
Let us rouse the fire of his love.

The very thought of Gesar may delight
Or frighten, or repel us,
But it shakes us from pettiness and bias.

Always he comes into our minds
With passion, ferocity, daring and love.

So if one wishes to pray, one should do so.
If one wishes to practice fencing, archery, horsemanship, do it.
If one drinks, sings, ploughs, weaves, sings, makes love,
Do this in the way King Gesar himself has done:
Plunge into the uncertainty of awake.

Gesar's unconquerable radiance
Is the thread that binds us together
In this great pulse of life.

This is the thread that burns like fire,
And blazes from our great King's heart.

It binds us together in whatever our fate may be.

Tsashang Denma's song heartens the ministers, warriors and people of Ling, and as the days passed many indeed follow his advice. Day and night there are many who sit and pray before Gesar's tent. Daily, warriors drill and practice archery and swordsmanship. Farmers resume tilling the soil, children return to their lessons, craftsmen and women continue their work.

But day after day, Gesar lies on his bed, pale and inert, his breath shallow, and doubt begins to pervade Ling. Though everything seems normal, nothing feels that way. When warriors ride out across the plains, shouting the warrior cry as they spur their horses, the sounds of KI and SO remind them of their ailing king and echo hollowly. Late into the night, around campfires, they drink and try to rouse themselves, telling the stories of Gesar's many deeds. Women laugh and joke, but the thought of Gesar himself, ill and perhaps dying, suddenly punctures the merriment, smothers their laughter, and causes an embarrassed silence.

It is as if they had all been entranced as a great storyteller recounted a marvelous tale. But as the story is coming to its end, the audience is now uncomfortably aware that their experience, even if it is still continuing, has been just another kind of dream.

And so, Sechan Dugmo's song floats out into the cool air night after night and echoes the questions that haunt the unquiet sleep of everyone in the camp. In the deep night, a tired warrior dreams of Gesar in gleaming armor flailing his sword against hordes of demons. A young mother dreams of Gesar laughing in a white marble courtyard filled with the perfume of flowers and the play of fountains. A shepherd sleeping in the hills dreams of Gesar riding on the back of his great wonder horse, Kyang Ko Kar Kar at the head of a great herd of bison thundering across the grassy plains.

Meanwhile far away in the west, living as far from Gesar as he could while remaining in Ling, Lord Todong, Gesar's troublesome and often treacherous uncle has for many years been encamped in a high verdant valley. He lives there with his wife, his family, an entourage of warriors and servants and a lama, one Kunga by name, who renounced his vows and became Todong's principal drinking companion. The surrounding farms and Todong's great herds of horses, yak and dri provide for all their needs. In the midst of this encampment, which is in fact a small town, Todong manages local affairs but devotes most of his time to reminiscing and to windy philosophical speculations with his friend. He seems content enough with this quiet life, and many think that this is natural enough for a man moving towards old age.

But a messenger sent in secret by the Princes of Hor and Jang comes to him with word of the Lord of Ling's strange sickness. Soon thereafter he has a dream which he tells his wife, Kurzar Sartok.

"A dream, a vision. I stood on a mountain peak that rocked and swayed, and all around me, mountain ranges shook like storm-tossed seas. Thunderclouds swirled all about and sheets of lightning struck the earth in deafening crashes. It was as if all the elements were in chaos. There was only terror. Winds howled like tortured demons, gales shrieked like vampires, and thunder rolled like the deafening sound of maddened warhorses charging.

"I drew my sword, but there was nothing to attack and nothing to defend against. 'Show yourselves!' I cried, and suddenly I was in the midst of a dazzling bright void.

"All at once a great raven with wings as black as night, a beak of onyx, and eyes like depthless mountain pools flew up in front of me. He hovered before me and said in a voice that blared like a battle trumpet: ' Ling now summons you.'

'No,' I shouted, 'No, I have answered this call before, but it leads only to disaster. I shall not go to Ling again.'

"But then the crow lit softly on my shoulder and now in a beautiful melodic voice sang to me. 'All your suffering shall be repaid. Now is your time.'" Kurzar Sartok has heard this sort of thing many times before and replies sharply:

"You may have gotten old, but obviously nothing much has changed. You have not gotten wise. This is not the first time such crows have come to you after a night of drinking to stir up your aged but undiminished lusts." She sneers and turns her back on him.

"The empty radiance of wisdom shines out throughout the world and casts its shadows in our dreams. From the free play of light, visions arise. " Todong replies pompously.

"You can talk that way with your broken down lama crony, but please don't try it out on me," snaps Kurzar Sertog. Todong looks offended and complains:

"If the world had left me alone, had left my mind in peace, I would have remained ' in exile. But fate calls me back to my true home, and it cannot be denied." Then Todong interprets his dream in a song mixed of lament and pride:

Of all the beings of this age,
My lineage is of the best:
I am born from the mind of Hayagriva
Whose trumpeting cry
Proclaims the eight forms of wisdom.
That in my dream
I stood in the center of universal chaos
Proves this.

In this earth, I am the son of a king.
I am strong of body and swift of mind.
My warriorship is fearsome
And my strategies dazzling.
No one denies the truth of this.
Never have I lacked for wealth, for followers or attendants.
At any other time, I would have been a great man.
That I drew my sword in the midst of chaos and did not waver
Proves this.

And yet, like an uninvited and unwanted guest,
I have lived in the shadow of Gesar's life,
People now and in the future
Know and will know me only as
His antagonist and foil.
For this reason,
Thunder and lightening blinded me in the dream.

Despite my every effort,
Again and again, I have played this loathsome role.
And so I am exiled in history
As a figure of contempt in the sagas of the great hero.
This is why I was alone.

But now Gesar is dying.
His time is at an end,
And my time, at last, has come.
All others shall know me as I know myself to be.
The Kingdom of Ling shall be my kingdom.
And the history of Ling shall be my history.
This is why the world shook and rolled.

By lineage and birthright,
I am entitled to be the hero of my own story.
These are the raven's very words.

I, my family and heirs, and even you, dear wife,
Who have never given me a moment's peace,
Shall preside over a grateful and prosperous land,

And shine like the sun in the annals of time.
That stillness and light were restored
When I stood my ground
Shows that this is so.

Todong has no sooner finished his song than Kursar Sertog resumes berating him. "Everyone knows you are famous for your dreams and for interpreting them. But when you were right, you were unable to accomplish any benefit for anyone, and when you were wrong, you were humiliated." Todong hisses back at her:

"Well then, if that is how it is, if I am just a puppet in some malicious karmic joke, I have no choice but to play my part. That is what I am. Just as it seems to be my fate to have a wife who despises me." Kursar Sartog looks at her husband, tears begin to stream down her face, and in a low voice she sings this song:

When first I saw you,
You shone like a morning star.
When I first heard you speak,
Your words filled the air like fireflies in the night.
You were the promise of everything,
And I was proud to be your wife.

But you were fascinated by what was not yours.
You cast yourself as Gesar's rival.
Your mind and deeds have tracked only him.
He fills your heart, your mind, your life,
And there is no place for me
Except to share in your constant disgrace.

Then she looks at her husband and asks: "How could I speak to you in any other way?" and she sits down on the floor and weeps.

It takes Todong a while to compose himself and then, although it is the middle of the night, he sends his servants to summon his son, Nakchen Gyatso and his son's wife, the Shingti Princess, Methok Lhadze. He tells them of his plans to return to Ling and the part each of them should play. "Slowly and carefully," he tells them, "we shall draw people to our camp. They will soon turn to follow us."

"But the people of Ling despise you, my learned father." But Todong cuts him off.

"They have followed Gesar for his valor through years and years of war. Now they want peace and to follow a good religious man."

"You, a good religious man? Really!" sneers Kursar Sartog.

"Why not?" Todong smiles. "I've learned a few things from old Kunga. He was once an abbot, you know. But anyhow, it's not as hard as people think, once you've got the hang of it." Todong's wife sweeps out of the room, exasperated.

"But why should anyone believe this?" asks Nakchen Gyatso.

"You two will tell them, and they'll believe you because, well, you are so very generous," Todong smiles in reply.

As Nakchen Gyatso and his wife walk back to their tent beneath the pallid light of the half moon sinking into the West, his mind blazes. A long suppressed yearning becomes a vision before his eyes. Their exile in this remote place is now about to end. His father will rule. Then there will come a time when his father too is gone. Then he, Nakchen Gyatso will lead.

Freed from waiting, from politics, from diplomacy, he can see himself riding like a great wind across the trackless steppes, leading hordes of warriors into battle, clashing with huge armies, sacking walled cities. Ling could be a base for conquests that even Gesar or his father had never dreamed of, and it is a life of striving in battle that stirs his heart. Already he can imagine a maddened horse quivering under him; he can smell the smoke of burning towers and hear the roar of battle. Even now, his eyes bulge, his breath quickens, and his strides become longer.

Walking at his side, the beautiful Princess Methok Lhadze also finds herself excited. Years of attending to her spiteful mother-in-law, years of enduring Todong's gloomy posturing and trying to appease her husband's sullen frustration are about to change. It seems that a new and brighter horizon is opening before her. So, as she rides beneath the faint starlight of a deep and moonless sky, she sings this song:

Oh, I was a princess
Who once fell through the fiery air
And landed like a lotus flower
Into the hand of a conqueror.

He would not take me.
Now I hover in another's gaze.

Oh I am a princess
Who floats like a flower petal
In the shining air,
Forever tossed on the wind.

Dancing forever above the earth,
Like a flame in the wind,
I will dazzle those who take me to heart
And remember no other.

*

In The Body of Vajrasattva : The Six Realms

Now, Gesar, the Great Lion Lord and his horse of miracles, Kyang Ko Kar Kar descend into the body of Yama, Lord of Death. There they see the six realms arranged one below the other. This is sung in a swift staccato manner accompanied by hand drum and flute.

Gesar, King of Ling on the back of his great steed Kyang Ko Kar Kar flies like a shooting star, down and down through the darkness. Suddenly, horse and rider shear through an imperceptible membrane. In an instant beyond perception or comprehension, all the light in all inner and outer phenomena come together in a single centerless explosion of brightness.

Suddenly there is no Gesar, no Kyang Ko Kar Kar, no Lord of Death, no realms, no being. In this coruscating radiance, there is no direction, no time, no point of reference, nothing to experience, nothing to understand, and no one to experience or understand. Total light, inseparable from space, ceaselessly expanding and consuming itself, then unfolds as awareness in form and sound.

Like a vast sun rising from a blazing colorless sky,
The all-pervasive light of primordial awareness dawns
As pure presence.
This is the naked form of Vajrasattva.

He is white in color and suffused with light,
Seated at ease in the bright expanse of space,
Holding a golden dorje upright in his right hand
And a silver bell at his waist.

He fills the whole of space.
And encompasses everything.

Free from time, he is eternally youthful,
The origin and essence
Of the infinite paths of wakefulness.

Free from concept,
His smile is the light of compassion itself,
And his song is the inexhaustible echo of silence.

What is called Gesar
Is the Bindu of Vajrasattva.

What is called Kyang Ko Kar Kar
Is the Prana of Vajrasattva.

What are called the pure and impure realms of existence
Are the meeting of the nadis of Vajrasattva.

Gesar completely dissolves in the luminous purity of Vajrasattva's being. Between himself, the horse Kyang Ko Kar Kar and all the realms and all beings there is no separation, distinction or exclusion. All are absorbed in the vast, colorless radiance of empty awareness, even as space continues to unfold in a panoply of solid-seeming forms.

From the light of unborn space itself,
A spontaneous rainbow arises.
This is the mandala of unfabricated wisdom.

This is awake as the blue absolute of Dharmadhatu
Experienced as space.
This is awake as the white mirror-like expanse
Experienced as water.
This is awake as the yellow expanse of equanimity
Experienced as earth.
This is awake as the ruby expanse of discernment
Experienced as fire.
This is awake as the emerald expanse of completion
Experienced as wind.

Gesar experiences the inner nature of Vajrasattva's body as great discs of light one upon the other, shimmering in a limitless space of colorless radiance. At the level of Vajrasattva's head is bright blue light. At his throat is a disc of bright green light, and at his heart golden yellow light. At his navel is a swirling disc of rainbow light and below that, in his secret center, bright red light.

Clinging to the vividness of wakefulness as mind,
The Bindu of a mind is cloaked in beginning, perpetuation,
Dissolving, and in the void itself.

The six realms of being,
Perceived as separate dwellings and modes of life,
Appear as the space of the six senses,
And an infinity of illusory moments called beings.

An endless succession of moments:
By solidifying one and dwelling within it,
Being, realm, and time appear.

The space around Gesar and the Horse of Wind, Kyang Ko Kar Kar seems to become solid. Simultaneously, the body of Vajrasattva now appears as the body of the Lord of Death. Thus, horse and rider find themselves at the summit of the enormous space within the body of Yama, King of Death.

Below them, the six realms turn and shimmer like a great inverted whirlpool of light within the smoke of a burning pit. The light at the narrow summit of the whirlpool is clear and bright; but at its wide distant base, dim and sulfurous. As the realms oscillate in the interplay of life and death, a deep throbbing pulse, like the deep humming of a great beehive, fills the space within the Lord of Death.

In the all-inclusive mirror of primordial awareness,
All display, whether true or delusory,
Is the path of wakening.

Spinning onward in the pattern of the seasons
Prana, the movement of mind, exhausts all forms it animates.

In every moment of wakening
Something dies.

This is the inseparable body, speech and mind of Vajrasattva,
Appearing in the realms of existence as the body of the Lord of Death.

So riding on the wind of life, the noble stallion, the radiant Kyang Ko Kar Kar, Gesar, Lord of Warriors descend through the lights of the realms and enter them all without fear or hesitation.

They fall head over heels through the dark roaring air. The space around them becomes more dense and more painful. And as if they woke from fainting, they find themselves in the Realms of Hell at the level of the Lord of Death's secret center. Gesar summons his resolve and begins the search for his mother.

*

The Realm of Hell/ The Bardo of Death
This is accompanied by percussion.

Riding furiously, plunging through the roiling black sky, Gesar and the Miracle Horse Kyang Ko Kar Kar careen down into the deepest depths of Hell through flumes of vapor stinking with the scent of boiling excrement, burning flesh and hair.

They fly through scorching fiery air beneath a dense sky of oily clouds. They soar above volcanic mountains and between ravines of red-hot iron. They skim rivers and seas of boiling molten copper in the eight hot hells. They rise through the frozen darkness above the glacial plains of the eight cold hells. They speed through the four neighboring hells called glowing ember, swamp of corpses, path of razor blades, and the unfordable river.

They witness every form of dying that was ever inflicted, feared, imagined or endured. Their search seems endless. The hot hells are landscapes burning like the inside of a vast blacksmith's furnace, filled with armies of crazed beings locked in endless battle. Full of rage and fury, they cut, stab, beat, kick, shoot arrows, hack limbs and tear out the eyes of one another. Their screams of pain and howls of rage are unending.

But upon death, there is no loss of consciousness. Men, women and children are tortured, die and immediately resume living, their bodies whole. They are then tortured and killed again. Elsewhere, crowds maddened with terror run into red-hot mountain ravines, are crushed to death by flaming boulders, revive and race on.

In the cold hells, there is no sun or moon or source of warmth and no light at all. Beings there freeze to death in utter isolation. Desolate and alone, their skin splits, their teeth chatter and break, their bodies turn to ice and shatter. Their death is slow but their return to life is instant.

For all who dwell in Hell, the consciousness of suffering never wavers or abates. Their minds are occupied only with hatred of their circumstance and an unrelieved desire to end it. Death is the only liberation that they know, and they yearn for it even as they fear it. But in dying, they experience only pain without release or alteration in their states of mind. Like living puppets pushed and pulled on burning iron rods, their fear of losing consciousness of themselves and their rage at all that seemed to frustrate them create ever greater and more horrific torments.

There is no place where Gesar and his steed can escape seeing all the most intense and grotesque kind of torture and death. They cannot shield their minds from the horrors and cries around them. Everywhere is whimpering, screaming and wailing, and smoke, the stench of excrement and burning flesh. Gesar and his great horse of miracles think they will go mad. And though they search, they cannot find Gesar's mother in any of the heaps of corpses and the faceless hordes of those still living.

Then as if hearing a distant bell somewhere in a hurricane, Kyang Ko Kar Kar hears Gesar's mother's far off cry. Pricking up his ears, he lunges into the smoky darkness, and following her voice, he and his rider find her in the Hell called Swamp of Corpses.

Thinking that she could escape from the fields of burning embers into which she had wandered, Dzeden has made her way to a great marsh choked with the rotting bodies of humans, pigs, cattle, horses and other animals. But as she entered the waters of the swamp and sank up to her shoulders, maggots, worms and insects with small pin-sharp teeth began to shred her skin and flesh. Pressed by hordes of people behind her, she was forced to continue on, surrounded by mobs of tortured screaming beings.

Nothing is left in her ravaged blackened form or contorted features that resembles the one whom Gesar had loved. Even so, he somehow recognizes her. Dropping through the smoke and fire, as if one the back of an eagle, he descends and hovers in the air before her.

Furiously he draws his great crystal sword and hacks at the serpents feasting on the struggling corpses to clear a path for her. But his sword has no effect and makes not even a ripple in the ooze surrounding Dzeden. Still he cannot stop slashing. His eyes are wet with tears; he wants to sob, and finally he cries out:

"Mother, you need suffer no more. I will take you from this place." Looking up, Dzeden howls and dives down into the suppurating mass. Unwilling to face the terrors above the surface of the swamp but unable to breathe and bleeding from wounds over her entire body, soon she dies. Gesar waits; when he sees the bubbles where his mother had vanished cease, he wants to die. But Dzeden then floats up through the foul greenish waters, gasps, and continues struggling. Gesar, overcome with horror, calls out to her again and hovers closer, holding out his hand. But again, Dzeden shrieks with rage and terror.

"Demon. Hell demon," she screams and plunges again beneath the morass of rotting and half-dismembered bodies. Again she dies and is reborn in the very same place. Again she sees Gesar waiting for her, and this time she tries to swim away. But with every stroke flesh is ripped from her arms and neck and chest, and blood spurts from a hundred cuts and bites.

Gesar realizes that his mother sees him as one of the many tortures of Hell and cannot see him in any other way. So when she next emerges revived from that swamp of perpetual death, he swoops down and swings her up onto Kyang Ko Kar Kar's back.

Dzeden fights, biting and kicking at him, hissing and spitting all the while. Her fetid breath smells like a decaying corpse. The lower half of her body had been half eaten away, festering and smelling of feces, pus, and rotted flesh. And Gesar, as he wrestles to keep his hold on her, wonders if this tortured being has retained any vestige of the gentle woman who had once rocked him in her arms and sung to him.

Gesar spurs Kyang Ko Kar Kar. The miracle horse, a trail of sparks falling from his steel hooves, rises high into the air until they hover in a still place as if they have found the eye of a tornado above the very center of hell. Jets of flames, molten lava, cinders, and an ear-shattering roar swirl all around without touching them. Below them lies a vast fiery pit in which the eight hells rest one atop the other. Around the pit are ranged the eight cold hells, and around them the eight neighboring hells. Everywhere Gesar and his great steed look, there is nothing but torment and pain. There is only the sound of hacking and burning and screaming. There is only the smell of fresh blood, rot and excrement.

And while they hover in a steaming vortex of horror and suffering, they feel their own bodies being crushed, burned, frozen and flayed as if they themselves are dying. Gesar and Kyang Ko Kar Kar feel as if once again they are locked in battle with Lutzen, the twelve-armed Demon Lord of the North.

And yet they are suspended in a bright shaft of motionless pale air which sinks beneath them through the circles of hell and rises above them into a bright space they cannot penetrate.

Dzeden screams and moans, writhing to escape from her son's grasp. Gesar cannot separate himself from all this inner anguish and outer pain, but he holds his mother tight and whispers to her:

Listen mother and be still.
Only if you can let yourself die
And not hold to this mind you think is you,
Will there be any freedom.

Dzeden gives no sign of hearing but she looks puzzled; her struggle lessens. Gesar, encouraged, says to her: "Now though what I tell you may make no sense within your maddened mind, I pray that my song will impress itself within your heart. This is something you must know." And so he sings:

Here we are poised in the radiant emptiness of the central channel,
The avadhuti of the Lord of Death,
The inner path of Vajrasattva:
This is the luminous pathway of the bardos.
Nothing here can be eluded or grasped.
Here is the display of enlightenment as complete duality.

All that is called existence, being or realm,
Whether as hell being or hell,
Hungry ghost, animal, human, Asura,

God realm or god
Is inseparable from the all-encompassing continuum called bardo.

Because no realm is permanent
And no occupant there stable,
There can never be anything other
Than this transitional state.

This continuum devoid of rest,
Is known by these signs:

Within the current of bardo
All experience flows
Between subjective and objective poles.

Here is the endless continuum
Of subjective grasping,
Which produces the illusion of the desire realm.

Here is the endless continuum
Of objective fixation,
Which produces the illusion of the form realm.

Here is the endless continuum of absorption
Whose illusion of non-duality produces the formless realm.

Within all these,
The experience of having an independent self within a stable realm
Is momentary.

Because all realms are mere islands
In the luminous river of the bardo states,
All subjective experience is marked by incompleteness,

All objective experience by insufficiency,
And the two together by impermanence.

All experience within the stream of the bardos
Is unappeasable momentum,
As beings seek to confirm themselves

And shape their realms,
Or free themselves, or liberate all.

This velocity arises as the five poisons:
Aggression, pride, desire, envy,
And all-pervasive ignorance.

Thus the ceaseless continuum of bardo
Moves invariably through stages:
Existence, which contains the bardos of dream and meditation,
Death which is the reunion of mother and child luminosity,
The bardo of illusory body which is the gate of dharmata,
And the bardo of becoming which leads to birth and existence

Taking one or another of these states as the essence of reality,
Clinging to it with passion or aggression, pride or envy,
The six realms appear,
Like illusory islands in a raging stream.

In Hell you solidify the bardo of death.
Fear of dying, fear of losing some last shred you can call yourself,
Raging to maintain consciousness,
You perpetuate the tortures of death endlessly.
You have sustained your being by your own agony.

Now you must see this and enter the great stream,
The unending river of consciousness,
The infinite stream of the bardos
Which is formless, completely clear, does not cease,
And cannot be possessed.

    Holding his mother firmly with one arm, he points down. Reluctantly, she finally turns her head. She gazes into the realms of Hell, and it seems that the two of them hover there forever.

    The panorama of suffering and torture in Hell evoke in the minds of Gesar, Dzeden and Kyang Ko Kar Kar innumerable lifetimes of suffering and dying. They recall their numberless passages of rage and terror that lead only to a multitude of agonies and deaths. They feel themselves swept up in numbing anger. They remember the terrible agonies and deaths that afflicted those they had loved, those who were their friends, those whom had been their mortal enemies, those who were mere acquaintances and those of whom they had only heard. The inescapable universe of anguish and extinction fill their hearts and senses. They begin to weep and cannot stop.

As Gesar floats in the air, he feels himself die, wracked by pain and consumed by sorrow. He feels the solid and all encompassing panoply of Hell. He sees every torture and every instant of consciousness there spray up into the air as if a volcano is spewing a huge fan of molten glass. And all the beings in all of Hell glitter and burn, swirl slowly together, and coalesce.

All the firelights in all of Hell fuse together before him in a single mirror-like surface that slowly cools. It becomes one vast reflective surface, glowing with still, clear, white light of unchanging, all-pervasive mirror-like awareness. Gesar feels he is dissolving. Blinded, powerless and uncomprehending, he is immersed in a sea of unsparing white light. It seeps between all the atoms of his being, stripping away his flesh, melting his bones, and vaporizing all thought.

Consciousness and even pain itself dissolve into the light of pure awareness, as one by one all the realms of Hell are dissolved in brilliant white light. All of Gesar's mind and existence become the white light of Mirror-like Wisdom, dazzling, clear, and completely penetrating.

This is the light in the body of all the Buddhas. It is the pure essence of the element of water. It is the Eastern pure realm of Abhirati, Complete Joy which blazes from the heart of the immovable vajra being, Vajrasattva-Akshobhya.

Gesar's mind dissolves into the center of this realm, as the completely clear Mirror-like Wisdom of the awakened state. He appears in the form of Vajrasattva-Akshobhya, white and gleaming like a snow peak. He holds a crystal five-pointed dorje in his right hand and sits upon the back of a white battle elephant. He embraces his consort, Buddha Locana and is accompanied by the Bodhisattvas Ksitigharbha and Maitreya, Lasya and Puspa. The air around them is bright, cool and peaceful. All who dwell in this fortunate realm are unencumbered by the temporary circumstances of body, location and consciousness. Their awareness pervades the whole of space.

In this form, Gesar shimmers in space. Kyang Ko Kar Kar emits a great trumpeting neigh, but Dzeden, still stupefied with terror, shields her eyes from the blazing light. Then in a bright melodious voice, Gesar sings this song:

HA
As ice dissolving
In a still turquoise lake,
All momentary identity,
All divisions and limits
And known as anger

Dissolve on the radiant mirror,
Dissolve on the single point.
Dissolved and engulfed
In a boundless lake of peace.
AH AH AH

Then Gesar, King of Ling, his mother, Dzeden the Naga Princess, and his fearless Horse of Wind, Kyang Ko Kar Kar dissolve in all-pervasive white light as if vanishing in an empty mirror. And at that moment, for an instant, free from time, all the beings in Hell experience complete liberation.

*

The Realm of the Hungry Ghosts/ The Bardo of Becoming
This is accompanied by the sound of reeds.

The brilliance of the infinite expanse of pure white light shimmers and then reverberates in waves. A sense of movement begins to unfold. Consciousness, like an inexhaustible cosmic wind, insatiably seeks an object. Carried on this momentum, Gesar, Dzeden, and the horse of Wind, Kyang Ko Kar Kar find themselves moving in the Bardo of Becoming and enter the Realm of the Pretas, the Hungry Ghosts.

Below them, under a flat yellow sky is a beautiful land of clear streams, and cool lakes surrounded by orchards filled with ripe peaches, apples, pears, cherries, apricots and other kinds of fruit. Golden fields of barley, wheat and corn sway in gentle breezes. Squash, melon, beans, ground nuts and many other kinds of edible plants grow freely and in great abundance.

As they explore this land, the sight of so much food reminds Gesar and Kyang Ko Kar Kar of their own hunger and thirst. Even Dzeden, though still writhing and hissing, stops to look hungrily at the land below and begins to salivate. But as they descend, they smell the odor of rotting food and see the inhabitants of that realm hovering and darting, in groups or alone, like clouds of dust and smoke across the landscape.

These creatures all have enormous bellies like great air-balloons and shrivelled fragile limbs like dead blades of grass. They have huge red-rimmed eyes, mouths the size of pin-holes and throats the size of a single horse hair. As they approached clear water, it turned to pus and blood before their eyes. Sometimes, as they are about to eat fruit or grain, it withers at their touch and turns to dust before they put it in their mouths. At other times, fruit turns to stone and grain to sand. Whatever they manage to eat by day, turns by night to molten lead in the Preta's stomachs and prevents them from any rest.

Their minds are consumed with endless, unappeasable and rapacious hunger that nothing can satisfy or end. But as much as their own appetites torment them, the thought that another might be satisfied plagues them more. Even if an apple turns into a burning rock, they will not let it go for fear another will take it. Even knowing the pain it causes, they eat all they can to prevent others from having it. There is no instant in which they are satisfied. They know only continuous craving uninterrupted by sleep or dream. Some Pretas fly to higher realms where they seek to afflict the beings there with their own suffering. But even this brings no relief from their constant wanting. Existence and craving are for them inseparable. Chained to an unbreakable succession of desires, the Pretas do not experience death. Only by sheer exhaustion do their bodies finally disappear.

In the center of the Preta realm, sprawled on a granite mountain, lies the Queen of the Hungry Ghosts, larger than all the rest. Her belly is vast as a small city, and her limbs like water pipes stretch down the mountain. Her eyes are pools of blood, and her sparse gray hair drifts in the air like smoke from a brush fire. Her mottled gray skin is burned by the moonlight and frozen by the sun. From her tiny mouth comes a loud sucking sound, and in a moaning keening voice, repeating the same words over and over, she sings this song:

By day, I bear five hundred boys,
By night five hundred girls.
I eat them all before they cry,
And still I am not satisfied.

Gesar and the horse of miracles begin to rise and leave that place, but Gesar's mother cries and weeps. She pulls at Gesar, points to the rich lands below and smacks her lips. The sight of this realm's bounty has made her hungry, and she cannot bear to leave. But as they float in the sky, the ghosts below them look up and see horse and riders as great haunches of roast meat dangling just out of reach. Gnashing their teeth and smacking their lips, they leap and gasp and scream in frustration. Gesar shakes his head and wants to continue on, but his mother cries and holds him back. So Gesar sings this:

Here, poised in the luminous emptiness of the central channel,
We float in the avadhuti of the Lord of Death,
The inner path of Vajrasattva.
This is the luminous pathway of the bardos,
The natural union of duality and non-duality.
Nothing here can be eluded or grasped.

Born on the momentum of mind itself
Endlessly seeking an object,
You hover in the Preta Realm, the realm of Hungry Ghosts.
In the endless continuum of bardos
This realm and those who dwell here arise
From solidification as the Bardo of Becoming.

Desiring to establish your own being completely,
Only the world around seems real.
You yourself become a ghost.

Craving reality
Within and outside yourself,
You are never satisfied
And you can never stop.
Relying on the momentum of craving, nothing ever seems real.

Abandon want,
And enter the great stream of reality itself,
The endless succession of the bardos,
Which is formless, abundant and does not cease,
And cannot be possessed.

Gesar cannot tell if his mother understands him as she stares longingly at the panoply of temptations that extend below them. She does not seem to see the desperation of the ghostly beings who fly across this world in perpetual dissatisfaction. Slowly Gesar, Dzeden and the great wind horse all succumb to thirst and hunger. They feel as if they were once again struggling against the power of Satham of Jang, Demon Lord of the West. They remember countless lifetimes spent burning in the flames of desires, needs, and wants and as many lifetimes sunk in the sorrow of miserliness and frustration. They remember the lives of many loved ones, enemies, friends, and beings whom they had only known casually whose lives have been similarly deformed by avid lusts and whose worlds were similarly rendered a wasteland. Universes of longing and desire fill their minds, and visions of unattainable satisfaction overwhelm them, as they whirl in the inner fires of the Realm of Hungry Ghosts.

Gesar feels he is being consumed in the feverish momentum of craving and his mind is filled with desires, needs and yearnings. At the mere idea of something he could want, his body burns with fever, and his mind moves though all solid obstacles and flies vast distances. But when he nears some place of imagined peace or delight, he passes through it too. Nowhere can he stop, find any satisfaction, or rest or ease. The world around him is like a flickering bonfire, and he himself is like a dead leaf, itself, rising and falling, tossed and carried by gusts of flaming air.

Gesar swirls and burns helplessly in the flames. His passions become nothing other than the hallucinatory totality of the Preta Realm and its occupants, consuming themselves in a great pyre of burning sparks and flashes. And slowly the points of light, all the illumination, the essence of the Preta Realm swirl together, fusing into a plane of scorching red light, filling and consuming the whole of space.

All desires and dissatisfactions and the pain of them are incinerated in this blazing red light. One by one all cravings and all objects of desire are burned up. All of Gesar's mind and being become the all-pervasive red light of Discriminating Awareness Wisdom, ceaseless, all- embracing and all- consuming.

This ruby light, the light of Discriminating Awareness Wisdom, is limitless great compassion, the light of the speech of all the Buddhas. It is the pure essence of the element of fire. It is the Western pure realm of Sukhavati, the Blissful, which expands from the heart of Amitabha, Boundless Light.

Then within the center of this realm, the all-embracing Discriminating -Awareness Wisdom of the awakened state, Gesar's heart is utterly consumed and rises in the form of Amitabha, red as a ruby and brilliant as the noon-day sun. He holds a white and red-tipped lotus in his right hand and sits upon the back of a peacock in full plumage. He embraces his consort, Pandaravasini and is accompanied by the Bodhisattvas Avalokitesvara and Manjusri, Gita and Aloka. The air around them is warm and accepting. All who have the good fortune to dwell in this realm are not limited by the temporary circumstances of body and location. Their compassion radiates throughout all the realms and all the bardos to where ever it is needed.

In this form, Gesar radiates throughout the whole of space, and in a voice like a hot wind he sings to his mother and to Kyang Ko Kar Kar, his faithful companion.

NI
As a rotting corpse
Is consumed by a fragrant fire,
All momentary identity
All craving for me and mine,
All obsessions and projections
Experienced as desire
Are consumed by the fire
Of great compassion;
Consumed and satiated
In the boundless flame
Of universal love.
AH AH AH

So are Gesar, King of Ling, his mother, Dzeden the Naga Princess, and his fearless Horse of Wind, Kyang Ko Kar Kar consumed utterly in the heat of all-encompassing love. And at that moment, for an instant free from time, all the beings in the Preta Realm experience complete liberation.

*

The Animal Realm/ The Bardo of Dream
This is accompanied by single stringed instruments.

Within the swirling flames of the expanse of ruby light, shapes and images rise and fall. Visions that seem completely real appear and just as suddenly vanish. It is impossible to tell what is imaginary and what is not, but the desire merely to survive is overwhelming. Thus Gesar, Dzeden, and Kyang Ko Kar Kar find themselves moving in the Bardo of Dream, and so enter the Animal Realm.

Beneath a dull green sky, a vast terrain of seas, rivers, lakes, swamps, grassy planes, dense forests, jungles, deserts, wooded hills, and sheer rock mountains stretch below them. Throughout this realm live many kinds of animals. Beneath the seas, some in lightless depths and some near the water's sparkling surface, swim enormous whales and marlin, squid, sharks and great flashing schools of smaller fish, feeding on still smaller life forms: shrimp, krill and clams, and on each other.

Under the earth, an infinite number of insects burrow and build great cities. Many rodents dig long twisting tunnels to hide their nests. On the surface of the earth roam vast herds of cattle, bison, deer and horses, packs of wolves, tigers, bears, lions, elephants, and many others. High in the trees are clans of monkeys, lemurs and apes. Above the earth fly flocks of wild birds, waterfowl, parrots, finches, sparrows, grackles, ravens, and smaller groups of eagles, hawks, and vultures.

Throughout this realm, pervading it and living even inside every animal, are colonies of microscopic life forms beyond numbering. They live consuming each other and in utter terror of being consumed. Puppets of instinct, ignoring and ignorant of all other possibilities, unable to change the focus of their lives, their consciousness is completely immersed in the requirements of survival.

Animals, comforted by the rank scent of their own kind, move in vast migrations, snorting, bellowing, roaring screeching, buzzing, above the earth, across its surface, and beneath its seas to that end. There is no thought beyond the instinct to continue existing.

Those who live under human domination have this same impulse but find themselves subject to harsh usage and finally slaughter. Their only respite is in dreams where they gambol and feast and nuzzle in a warm place that finally is safe.

Kyang Ko Kar Kar, the swift wind of miracles again finds himself dozing. Gesar's mother, for the first time since Gesar plucked her from the swamp of hell, smiles. Gesar, touched to see his mother finally eased from her suffering and sorrow, hovers in that realm for many months. And as they drift across the sky, herds of beasts follow them. But for Gesar, this reminds him of his struggles in the dream-like realm of Shingti, Demon Lord of the South, so he rouses himself and sings to Dzeden:

You float in the avadhuti of the Lord of Death:
This is the luminous pathway of the bardos,
The inner path of Vajrasattva:
Nothing here can be eluded or grasped.
This is display of enlightenment as complete duality.

Ignoring everything not given by instinct,
Endlessly holding to the security of sleep and dream,
You wander in the Animal Realm.
In the endless continuum of bardos,
This realm and those who dwell here arise
From solidification the Bardo of Dream.

Believing that every flickering thought is solid,
Every wave of feeling true,
Following the path of every scent, sight, and sound,
Acting as if the world is solid,
As if oneself, one's kind and world would never end,
You live in the dream world of an animal.

Ignorant of cause or effect,
Unconcerned with anything beyond the immediacy of existing,
There is nothing beyond instinct and the givens of experience.

You do not know who you are
Or why you act or what world there is beyond sensation.
You are one with a dream world
Where there is neither knowledge nor change.

This solidity is an illusion which death will soon end.
Enter the great stream of reality itself,
The endless succession of the bardos,
Which is formless, unchanging, and does not cease:

The life beyond life,
It cannot be ignored.

Gesar, his mother and the noble steed all feel exhausted from the endless succession of visions and mental states through which they have been journeying. They long for a life that promises unchanging simplicity. But with this longing rise many memories of lives passed fearfully in the smallest compass, relying on simple instinct. There the race to gain the means of staying alive was relieved only by dreams. They remember many of their own lifetimes exhausted in this way. And they see the lives of those they had loved, feared, and had merely seen from afar passing through the same state. Eons of hiding in dark shelters, endless movement and the struggle simply to survive overwhelm them and render them speechless, as they float across the Animal Realm.

Gesar feels himself change with each scene below him. One moment he is courageous and bold, and the next completely afraid. He is cold, selfish and cruel, then suddenly anxious and loving. One moment he is dominated by fury and the next by rut. He burrows in darkness, then flies in the brightness of the sky. His body is huge, then minute, soft, then armored. He feels caught in a succession of dreams and is losing all contact with any stable reality. The world is unstable as a mirage. He can no longer distinguish between awake and asleep.

Then, Gesar, the entire Animal Realm and those who dwell there dissipate and diffuse like rushing banks of clouds covering the sky. Some are dark and turbulent like a coming storm, others like serenely glowing white towers, others still like extravagant sunsets and subtle dawns. Slowly all these clouds of light swirl together, blending in a vibrant stream of rainbow light that fills the whole of space.

This rainbow light, pervading the ten directions, is the unfabricated and indivisible mandala of the five lights, the five wisdoms and the five Buddha families together with all the wisdom holders, gurus, yidams and protectors.

In the center of this rainbow mandala, all Gesar's phenomena melt into the white light of Dharmadhatu Wisdom of the pure awakened state as Buddha Vairocana. He then appears with his consort and retinue, clear and radiant, sparkling like a diamond in this realm, The All Pervading Circle.

At the Eastern gate of the mandala of the All Pervading Circle, he appears simultaneously from the blue light of all pervasive Mirror-Like Wisdom of the awakened state in the form of Vajrasattva-Akshobhya together with his consort and his retinue, blue as a sapphire and luminous as the hour before dawn in his realm, Complete Joy.

At the Southern gate of the mandala, he arises from the yellow light of the Wisdom of Equanimity in the form of Ratnasambhava with his consort and retinue, yellow as an ocean of gold in his realm, The Glorious. _

At the Western gate of the mandala, Gesar is consumed by the red light of all embracing Discriminating-Awareness Wisdom of the awakened state and appears in the form of Amitabha together with his consort and his retinue, red as a ruby and brilliant as the noonday sun in his Blissful Realm of Lotuses.

At the Northern gate of the Mandala of all the Buddhas, he rises from the emerald light of All-Accomplishing Wisdom of the awakened state in the form of Amogasiddhi together with his consort and retinue, emerald green like the light before a thunderstorm in his realm, Perfected Actions.

Towering clouds of wisdom holders, sages and wrathful dharma protectors, surround the awakened ones. The air is completely filled blazing discs of light and a cacophony of celestial melodies, thunder, shrill war cries, bells and drums. All notions of clinging to a self or a dwelling place are stripped away in the pure naked power of space itself. All the universes resounded with its melody.

KHAM

The great blazing sun
Leaves no shadow
There is no place to hide
And no place to dream of hiding.

All momentary identity,
All the struggle for survival,
All fears and dreams
Experienced as ignorance,
Vaporize in the inescapable brilliance,
The simplicity of awake:

Utterly dispelled,
Alive and free
In the unfettered display
Of life force itself.

AH AH AH

Gesar, Lion Lord of Ling of Ling, his mother, Dzeden the Naga Princess, and his fearless Horse of Wind, Kyang Ko Kar Kar disappear into the great display of unconditional wakefulness. And at that same moment, for an instant free from time, all the beings in the Animal Realm experience complete liberation.

*

The Human Realm/Bardos of Illusory Body and Dharmata
This is accompanied by flute, horns, and a tam-tam.

The all-pervasive display of rainbow light becomes more solid. Gesar, Dzeden and Kyang Ko Kar Kar feel their inner experiences becoming more concrete and irritating. They long to control their journey by using their intelligence and for situations that confirm the reality of their desires and intentions. But no matter how vivid, the things they encounter, this aim eludes them. Thus they journey in the Bardos of Illusory Body and Dharmata and enter the Human Realm.

Below a pale blue sky, the terrain and landscape differs from that of the animal realm only in the many alterations which humankind has made. Rivers are dammed near their source and directed into canals. At their mouths are great populous cities filled with temples, palaces, universities, market places, the houses of merchants and artisans and the hovels of the poor. Plumes of smoke rise from factories, turning out cloth, pottery, furniture, tools, weapons, and all manner of goods. Acres and acres of land have been turned into pastures, farms and orchards. Villages and small towns are everywhere. Paved and unpaved roadways mark the trade routes that crisscross all but the most inhospitable terrain. Nomads drive their herds across vast plains. Hunters track their prey through jungles and tundra. Mountains are honeycombed with mines. Ocean-going ships plow across invisible sea-lanes. Prayers, curses, laughter, tears and, sighs fill the air.

It is the nature of those in the human realm to live together, and they are capable of changing their immediate circumstances in accord with their desires and ideas. They use intellect to gain mastery over their phenomena. Passions and the thought forms they contrive to satisfy their desires or avoid their frustration dominate their minds. It is often impossible for them to distinguish between the reality of thoughts and the reality of the physical world. Their restlessness often causes them to wish to alter or abandon whatever circumstances in which they find themselves.

Because they are capable of changing their lives in accord with their aspirations, their imaginations are often stirred to emulate the examples of other realms. Some cultivate spiritual detachment and bliss, some revel in the luxury, power, and ease of gods, while others live in constant striving for such a way of life. Many however, like animals exploited by those who dominate them, struggle for survival and only dream of happiness; others have a life marked by unslaked craving; and still others are abandoned to a life of rage and crime in circumstances of violence and sudden death.

Dzeden stares down at this realm where she suffered so. Memories flood her mind as she watches the many lives of those who live there and she cannot decide whether to smile or sneer. But for Gesar and Kyang Ko Kar Kar, this world recalls the lures and artifices with which the Kingdom of Hor had ensnared the world, and so Gesar sings to his mother in a soft clear voice:

Suspended in the central channel of luminous emptiness,
We float in the avadhuti of the Lord of Death,
The inner path of Vajrasattva:
This is the luminous pathway of the bardos,
The natural union of duality and the awakened state.
Nothing here can be eluded or grasped.

Alternating between reality and unreality,
Projecting mental images of truth and bliss,
Striving to realize them,
Here you struggle in the Human Realm.
In the endless continuum of bardos
This realm and those who dwell here arise
From solidifying the Illusory Body and Bardo of Dharmata

Endowed with the powers of change,
Moved by waves of passionate longing, rage, fear, and despair,
Ideals, nostalgia and dramas shape and encase your perception,
You and the realm itself
Are constantly changing.

Creating systems of thought and action,
Following spiritual and secular paths,
Endowed with great intelligence and the power to change,
You seek to establish a reality that will not change.

Searching for the truth
In the mirror phantasmagoria of self and other
Here, you live in the relentless duality of the Human Realm.

This duality can never be resolved:
It is the display of that
Which is beyond duality and beyond mind.

So enter the great stream of reality itself,
The endless succession of the bardos,
Which is formless, filled with every quality, and does not cease:

The life beyond life,
It cannot be ignored.

Dzeden turns her face away and weeps. But as they hover above the Human Realm, a sensation born from a mixture of longing and happiness suddenly seizes Gesar's heart. He points to a place on the Northern border of the Southern continent that lies below them. "Look," he whispers urgently. "Look."

There, like a bright mirage hovering faintly above the rolling desert plains, stands a vast, glittering circular ring of snow covered mountains. Within it is an immense rich land, filled with emerald green fields and dense forests and divided into eight equal parts by broad silver streams. Each of these eight sections is a kingdom with its own traditions, capitol, villages, streams and lakes, pastures and farmland. This is the Kingdom of Shambhala.

At the center of this kingdom rises a high plateau surrounded by another ring of crystalline snow mountains. Near the center of the plateau, a large lake gleams like a sapphire. Behind it, at the very center of the kingdom, is the capitol city of Kalapa filling the sky with radiant golden light. This is the seat of the Rigden Kings who rule over all Shambhala from their great complex of palaces with cinnabar walls, carved golden pillars, and glittering crystal roofs and courtyards filled with laurel, cedar, peach, and cinnamon trees. Even from far away, Gesar, his mother and the Horse of Wind hear the distant chiming of the silver bells that adorn the eaves of the Kalapa Court. They smell the faint perfume of juniper incense. Gesar's heart is full of joy and he sings this song:

Hidden behind gleaming snow walls
Of solidified hope and fear: Shambhala.
Protected by ice towers
Of concepts about reality: Kalapa.
Its gateways are the senses themselves,
Free from the limitations of self-reference.

Ah, how the four great elements dance and shine
In the space of the Rigden's Imperial Mind,

Here, life, death and limitation
Are the pure ground.

Here the passions
Are the spontaneous light of wisdom.

Here duality
Is the living expression of non-duality.

Here the path of the Realms and Bardos
Is the path of awake,
Moving in every instant of light and darkness.

Here the heart of all human kind unfolds
In the fullness of its own love.

Here in the space of the Rigden's Imperial Mind.
Resting in the natural state,
Ordinary mind,
Suddenly free from the ice walls of fixed thinking
And the precipices of subconscious gossip,
The senses reform themselves.
The world reforms itself.

The virtues of the human realm rise here naturally
In the shape of the human heart,
In the shape of Shambhala.

So may all human beings see this living kingdom,
The home of the hearts of all,
The home of our heart.

Gesar is so deeply drawn to the vision of Shambhala that he is sure it must also be imprinted on his mother's mind, and they continue their journey in the human realm.

Endless chances for accomplishment, love, conquest, and gain fill the minds of the travelers. Gesar, Dzeden and the great wind horse all are exhilarated by the panoply of possibilities. But this spectacle brings with it the memory of many lives devoted to making mental projections real. They feel swamped in life after life wasted in this way.

All the pride in momentary accomplishments of mastery or rage at failures prevent those in the human realm from seeing that the painful experiences of birth, growing, old age, sickness and death cannot be manipulated or controlled. Gesar, his mother and his great steed remember the many lives of many loved ones, enemies, friends, and beings whom they had only known casually whose lives had likewise been spent in difficult struggle only to find a final revelation of their wasted efforts.

Gesar's mind becomes a deep well of sorrow as he senses that even his heroic human life has somehow been a trap. All his great battles, passionate loves, compelling intrigues, and triumphant exploits seem hollow. The tangible accomplishments of the kingdom of Ling will vanish in a generation. When he dies, all he brought to fruition will dissipate except as a story told for entertainment. In the end, he has merely been one of many actors in the unending theater of the Human Realm.

And as he gazes sadly into the vast expanse of human life, the ceaseless panoply of individual love, bravery, genius, treachery, splendor, cravenness, and self-deception and the longing from which it rises glow like reflections in a boundariless golden mirror.

Gesar is completely engulfed as all the innumerable inner and outer qualities of his life are absorbed like so many specks of dust into this expanse of dense, radiant golden light. His mind and existence became nothing other than the golden light of the Wisdom of Equanimity.

This is the light of the purified element of earth, the light of the infinite qualities of all the Buddhas. This is the Southern Pure Realm of Srimat, The Glorious that blazes from the heart of Ratnasambhava, the wish-fulfilling jewel.

In the center of this realm, from the all-sustaining Wisdom of Equanimity of the awakened state, Gesar's being rises in the form of Ratnasambhava, yellow as gold and radiant as the afternoon sun. He holds a wish-fulfilling jewel in his right hand and sits upon the back of a great golden horse. He embraces his consort, Mamaki, and is accompanied by the Bodhisattvas Akasagharba and Samantabhadra, Mala and Dhupa. The air around them is rich, honey-like and all-engulfing. All who have the good fortune to dwell in this realm are not limited by the temporary circumstances of body and location. Their generosity radiates throughout all the realms and all the bardos to wherever it is needed.

In this form Gesar blazes through the whole of space. Dzeden feels joy rise in her heart, and the miracle horse rears in the air. Then in a voice sweet and melodious, Gesar sings this song:

RI
As thoughts vanish
When rock meets bone,
All momentary identity,
All sense of inner possibility,
All outer perceptions taken to be real,
All such occasions for pride
Are absorbed into the golden ground
Of equal taste,
Absorbed and fulfilled
In the boundless qualities
Of the pure and fertile earth.
AH AH AH

So Gesar, King of Ling, his mother, Dzeden the Naga Princess, and his fearless Horse of Wind, Kyang Ko Kar Kar dissipate into utterly into the ever expanding amplitude of golden ground. And at that moment, for an instant free from time, every human being experiences complete liberation.

*

The Realm of the Jealous Gods/ The Bardo of Birth
This is accompanied by bass drums.

Adrift and exhausted amid the ceaseless permutations of dense golden light, Gesar, Dzeden, and Kyang Ko Kar Kar yearn to find some solid ground. But they are swept onward towards the Bardo of Birth, and enter the Asura Realm, the Realm of the Jealous Gods.

There, below a wine colored sky, wreathed in the smoke of forges and the scent of battle and fresh blood, the realm of the Asuras extends from the highest mountain flanks down into the deep canyons beneath the seas. The Asuras are warriors: their bodies are splendid and powerful and their life spans long. They are the inventors of fortified cities, and they live in splendor there amid their retinues of guards. Their treasuries are filled with gold and silver, all kinds of precious stones, intricate jewelry, and the choicest examples of the arts of other ancient and remote civilizations. Their libraries contain not only secret works on the arts of war and the construction of weaponry, but works from many realms on science, philosophy, politics, art, and precious spiritual teachings that have been otherwise lost.

Some of their cities stand on inaccessible snow peaks, others lower in broad grassy plains, and still others, those of the Naga Kings, lie beneath the rivers and seas. From their strongholds, the Asura lords join to conquer the realms of the Gods, but always they are defeated at great cost. Failing in the one endeavor that matters to them, they fight constantly with one another. They covet each other's territory, women, treasure, counselors, horses, weaponry, knowledge and reputation. Thus they form ever-shifting alliances; they hire unattached warriors and scientists, and send spies to gain momentary or more lasting advantages. Indefatigably, they direct all their studies and activities to this end. Thus the Asuras experience the great material, intellectual and spiritual gifts of their realm only as inadequate instruments which fail to achieve the dream, which is their only abiding reality.

In the Realm of the Gods, high above the Asuras but faintly visible at the apex of the purple Asura sky, grows a great Wish Fulfilling Tree. Effortlessly, this tree provides the gods with all they desire, be it any form of wisdom, power, wealth or sensual enjoyment. The roots of this tree run deep into the mountains and submarine chasms of the Asura realm. Knowing that this tree is always just out of reach, and seeing the greater splendor, power, and effortless pleasures of the gods who enjoy its fruit, the minds of all the Asuras are always filled with bitter envy. They cannot stop thinking of the pleasures and powers of the gods above them. They covet perfection and domination. Their discipline and exertion are unwavering. Their longing to be gods never abates. No possession, insight, friendship or thought has value unless it helps them to achieve this goal.

Gesar, his mother and his unfailing steed look down on the titanic struggles that churn the Asura realm. The Asuras' lofty ambitions remind them of many lifetimes expended in envious calculation and conflict. They re-live their own epic wars where no amount of prowess, foresight and nobility could assure a desired end. They remember the many lives of many loved ones, many enemies, many friends cut down in war. Gesar, Dzeden and Kyang Ko Kar Kar are awed by the sight of these great dramas playing out unceasingly over heaven and earth.

Dzeden's mind is stirred by the nobility of these great warriors and her heart swells with pride that she was once born to such a race. She yearns for the vigor of those who still have the good fortune to be among the living. Gesar holds her close and sings.

Rising in the central channel of luminous emptiness,
We float in the avadhuti of the Lord of Death:
This is the luminous pathway of the bardos,
The inner path of Vajrasattva.
Nothing here can be eluded or grasped.
This is display of enlightenment as complete duality.

Driven onward by the vision of an unchanging state,
Goaded on by the sight of the easy glory of the Gods,
Always aware of being groundless, incomplete,
You covet the power, bliss and splendor that you see beyond you.

Here, in the endless continuum of bardos,
The realm of the Asuras and those who dwell here arise
To solidify the Bardo of the Birth Place.

Calculating the advantages of one choice or another,
Strategizing to secure gain, plotting to avoid loss,
All your great powers of mind and body
Are devoted to the acquisition of a life just outside your reach.

Your life, power and attainments are never adequate.
Your endless ambition leads to ceaseless contest.

Your continual frustration burns and turns to bitter ash
As the promise of each birth and realm
Does not end the momentum of mind.

A mind of unceasing confrontation with the other
In pursuit of fulfillment
Is the shape of duality in the Realm of Jealous Gods.

Because this duality can never be resolved,
Surrender all goals and obstacles
And enter the great stream of reality itself,
The endless succession of the bardos,
Which is formless, complete and does not cease:
The life beyond life,
It cannot be ignored.

Still, Gesar feels a rush of exultant defiance as he flies above the Asura Realm. Careening through the smoke of battle, all around him arrows rain down and swords flash through the dark. Great chargers, hooves shaking the earth, race before him. The din of war cries, clashing swords, and screams of the dying are deafening. He is caught in thrashing storm clouds suffused with the dark green light that precedes a hurricane. And like a tornado breaking out of a summer sky, suddenly winds are raging in from all directions. The sheer momentum of the Asura's envious battle lust becomes a surging hurricane tearing through their realm. Every concept of self or other, every sense of real or unreal is stripped apart. There is only sulfurous light and unappeasable wind. Gesar's mind and being are completely dispersed, and he becomes nothing other than all-destroying, dark emerald light.

This is the light of the Wisdom of Completion, the light of the actions of all the Buddhas; the pure essence of the element of wind, the Wisdom of Absolute Completion of the awakened state. It is the expanse of the Northern Pure Realm, Prakuta, Accumulation of Actions.

In the center of this realm, Gesar's life force rises from the Wisdom of Completion in the form of Amogasiddhi, green and radiant as an emerald. He holds a crossed dorje in his right hand and sits upon the back of a black eagle with iron beak and talons soaring in the sky. He embraces his consort, Samaya-Tara and is accompanied by the Bodhisattvas Vajrapani and Sarvanivaranaviskambhin, Gandha and Naivedya. The air around them is sharp and electric. All who have the good fortune to dwell in this realm are not limited by the temporary circumstances of body and location. Their actions radiate throughout all the realms and all the bardos to wherever they are needed.

Dzeden and Kyang Ko Kar Kar are stupefied, and in a voice sharp as a crack of lightning, Gesar sings.

SA
The whirling black wind of time
Rips from the roots
All momentary identity,
All ideals,
All conceptual formations
Based on comparison.
They disappear in the movement of empty air.

The pure action of wind
The pure action of life force
Leaves no residue
And no memory.
AH AH AH

So, for an instant, all the movements of Gesar, King of Ling, his mother Dzeden the Naga Princess, and his fearless horse of wind, Kyang Ko Kar Kar spin apart. They are dispersed completely. And at that moment, for that instant free from time, every being in the Realm of the Jealous Gods experiences complete liberation.

*

The Realm of the Gods/ The Bardo of Meditation
This is accompanied by stringed instruments.

The infinite field of torrential and overwhelming energy is so utterly unsettled that the longing for a state that is permanent, blissful and at peace soon takes root in Gesar, his mother, Dzeden, and the great horse of wind, Kyang Ko Kar Kar. Thus they move in the Bardo of Meditation and entered the Realm of the Gods.

They spin up through pearl white air to the highest part of the Lord of Death's form. Slowly a great opalescent spiral of shimmering light, brilliant at the base and so refined as to be almost invisible at the peak, rises before them. Surrounded by a glowing matte white sky, the many kinds of Gods of the Desire Realm live around the lowest part, above them the Gods of Form, and at the apex dwell the Formless Gods. All abide in evolving the perfection of union.

The Gods of the Desire Realm live in ascending levels: some have power over phenomena in the lower realms; others dominate them. Regardless of their status,

CROSSINGS ON A BRIDGE OF LIGHT

the radiance and beauty of the gods and goddesses make them all irresistible and powerful. Their bliss and delight is all consuming. Because they live in a desire realm, they require companionship, dwellings, food and clothing to sustain their existence, but each and every desire is fulfilled as it arises. Thus they live in immense palaces of jeweled light filled with every beautiful thing, with perfume, music, and food, and attended by hosts of consorts, warriors and attendants. Surrounding these are gardens, parks, pleasure groves, pools of sapphire water and lakes of crystal.

Their thoughts are simultaneous with their deeds, and their desires are simultaneous with their satisfactions. They are utterly absorbed in the enjoyment of their own forms, powers, pleasures, and magnificence. There is no gap or interruption in their rapture, and they are utterly unaware that this will eventually end.

Gesar and his mother are lost in wonder at this vast and shining realm. There at the summit of the realm of the thirty-three gods, is the Diamond Palace of Brahma, shining like the light of the sun and moon together. From within it they hear the silvery voices of his consorts, filled with love and adoration, singing to him.

When Brahma, Lord of Space,
Creates all beings in the past present and future,
Their lives all take shape within his mind.

He has harnessed the forces within his being to create them.
Earth is the stability of his being.
Water, the fertility of his being.
Fire, the intensity of his being.
Air, the movement of his being.

Goodness rises within his memory.
Craving rises within his passion.
Generosity rises within his expanse
Light shines from his eyes.

The minds of beings arise
Within the primordial power of his speech.
Death and darkness are his sleep.

Gesar and his mother hear this and look out on this realm: no imperfection is visible in the life of the gods. But they see when a god's life span is coming to an end, he or she becomes stupefied with terror. For gods die suddenly. Suddenly, they no longer enjoy their palaces, their consorts, or their thrones. They are restless. Their scent becomes unpleasant, their food dissolves before they eat it. Their friends suddenly shun them. Their splendor fades like a flower petal in hot sun. They die in five short days in an agony of regret and sorrow, and it is this state of mind that determines the rebirth which now they seek desperately.

As Kyang Ko Kar Kar drifts higher, they now see the abode of the Gods of Form. These gods have no need of bodies nor palaces, nor a great panoply of powers and delights. Free of desire, they live in the limitless absorbtions of pure perception, contemplating the four great elements of wind, fire, water, and earth: green, red, blue, and yellow; sounds of the vowels and consonants; warmth and cold; the texture of old stones, of ice; the elemental shapes of triangles, spheres and cubes. Unwavering contemplation of perception constitutes their realm and being.

The meanings, textures, properties, implications, tones and extensions of these forms consume them utterly. Action and acquisitiveness are alien to them, and they live in a state of blissful fascination. They experience themselves and the objects of their fascination as inseparable and completely pure. They are themselves red, the sound Oh, a silver orb. Their change of state occurs only as a thought flickers into their absorption, or as a desire for some more solid or complex experience beyond absorption touches their mind.

Finally Gesar, Dzeden and the Horse of Miracles rise to the summit of existence, the apogee of all the realms of life and death, the realm of the Formless Gods. The gods here, not considering themselves to be alive or dead or capable of any alteration, live endlessly through eons. They exist only as meditative mental states inseparable from the objects of their meditation. Here subject and object are experienced as one, and there is no conception of other in any form. In this way, the gods abide in one of four states of increasing abstraction: consciousness as infinite space, infinite consciousness, consciousness as neither discernment nor non-discernment, and consciousness as nothing whatsoever.

These gods are completely absorbed and are themselves the pristine qualities of mind and space itself. For such subtle beings however, a single thought of any kind becomes immediately solid. The pure abstraction of their state of mind quickly becomes denser, and they descend suddenly into cruder forms of being. The birth and realm in a flickering imagining is then their life.

Gesar, Dzeden, and Kyang Ko Kar Kar float in an uninterrupted radiance where neither time nor space has any bearing. Gesar recalls all the moments in his life when it appeared his struggle might be ended, accomplishment might be final, and all the moments of peace and satisfaction might be eternal. Moments of rapturous contemplation at sunrise and hours when he meditated as all the troubled world dissolved into a luminous sky all come back vividly to mind. But his mother stirs in her sleep, and with a feeble gesture tries to ward off some dream creature. He looks at her and sings:

Rising to the summit of the central channel of luminous emptiness,
We rest in the avadhuti of the Lord of Death:
This is the luminous pathway of the bardos,
The inner path of Vajrasattva,
The natural union of duality and the awakened state.
Nothing here can be eluded or grasped.
This is display of enlightenment as complete duality.

By perfect concentration,
As the perceiver is absorbed into the perceived,
The thinker into thought,
The gods and their realms arise
Relying on luminosity within the Bardo of Meditation.

Living in the power of time
As the lords of past present and future;
Living in the intensity of the passions
As the gods of love and war, art and science;
Living in the vitality of earth, of water, of fire, of air,
As the gods of mountains, plains, seas, rivers, flame, and wind;
Living as the radiance of sight, sound, scent, touch, taste and cognition;
Living as the limitlessness of space, consciousness, emptiness, and equipoise,
They prolong those moments into eternity.

Because they are one with the moments in which all beings arise,
They have power over them.
Perfect in their absorption,
The plight of those below rarely moves them.

Though they experience the freedom from any limit,
Their eternity is still the endless continuum of the bardos.

Because they cultivate non-duality
As a state apart from duality,
Their end comes with insidious suddenness.

Duality can never be resolved
But is itself the display of that which is beyond duality and beyond mind.
So enter the great stream of reality itself,
The endless succession of the bardos,

Which is formless, pure and does not cease:
The life beyond life cannot be ignored.

Even merely hovering on the periphery of the various god realms is so intoxicating that neither Gesar nor his mother nor Kyang Ko Kar Kar can tell if one second has passed or many lifetimes.

The infinite expanse of cloudless radiance evokes in their minds many times of unobstructed ease and many moments of bliss, terminated with incomprehensible suddenness. They become one with the beauty, invulnerability and transcendent joy which has marked, however momentarily, the lives of many they have loved, some who were their friends, some whom who were mortal enemies, some who were mere acquaintances and some of whom they had only heard. The completeness of their bliss fills the travelers' hearts and floods their senses. They weep that it has now come to an end.

Amid the iridescent panoply of the God Realm, Gesar's mind and being is completely absorbed in unobstructed bliss and all pervasive, objectless consciousness. He is free from awareness of the sufferings of all the other beings and all the other realms and is, as well, free from his own past sufferings and struggles. He is free from alteration and time.

From within the soft and blissful luminosity of all the beings of the gods and their realms and from space itself, a clear blue light the color of sapphire appears. Beginning first as pinpoints of light, it expands like the sky, encompassing and dissolving all of samsara and nirvana, all inner and outer phenomena and the distinction between them. Its primordial pure radiance fills the whole of space with uncompromising empty blue light. Gesar is blinded, deafened, loses all feeling, and consciousness. All that remains is measureless indestructible space.

This blue light is the pure element of space, the Dharmadhatu Wisdom, the dazzling, clear and unsparing light of the mind of all the Buddhas. It is the Central Pure Realm, Abhirati, the All Pervading Circle.

Appearing in center of this realm, the Dharmadhatu Wisdom of the awakened state, Gesar is completely absorbed in the form of Vairocana, blue as a sapphire flame and subtle as the light before dawn. He holds the golden eight-spoked wheel of dharma in his right hand and sits upon a lion throne. He embraces his consort, Akasha Dhatvishvari, the Queen of Space. The air around them is bright, vibrant, implacable, and frightening. All who dwell in this fortunate realm are unencumbered by the temporary circumstances of body and location, and Buddha Nature itself pervades the whole of space. Then without thought or utterance, there is this song:

AH
Everything fabricated by mind,
All grasping and fixation,
Whether gross or subtle,
Are destroyed in the light of reality,
Which is the nature of space itself:

All momentary identity,
All deceptions and delusions
Experienced as self or other

Are dispelled in the light of space,
Are purified in non-meditation:

There is nothing to achieve, destroy or maintain
In the boundless expanse of reality itself.
AH AH AH

So Gesar, King of Ling, his mother, Dzeden the Naga Princess, and his fearless horse of wind, Kyang Ko Kar Kar are liberated from all deceptions within the circle of space, and they rise into the crown of Vajrasattva. At that same moment, for an instant free from time, all the beings in the God Realm whether of desire, form or formlessness, experience complete liberation.

*

Now from where they float at the summit of Vajrasattva's vast crystalline form, Gesar, Dzeden and Kyang Ko Kar Kar look down into a luminous expanse of milky light. There, within this, the six pure realms ascend from the pure intentions of the Awakened Ones. From them, rays of blue, white, red, yellow and green lights blaze. Haunting melodies and sudden insights pulse in the air. And surrounding these realms are innumerable others, some large as galaxies of stars and others faint and fleeting as aromas, all filling the body of Vajrasattva with uncountable multi-colored points of light.

Then slowly, these lights darken. The realms below them change color and congeal. The six pure realms now appear as the six realms of being: hot, smoky, roaring like a foundry and emitting odors which range from rot, sweat and blood, to dense floral perfume. And surrounding them are also many other realms, variations of the six principal ones, each buzzing like a wounded insect. The darkness gathers in the space around them until it is pitch black. Gesar, his mother and his noble steed find themselves again at the crown of the head of Yama, Lord of Death.

They do not move, and again slowly, the form of Yama fades to become the clear form of Vajrasattva. Likewise; the realms within lose their solidity and return to their radiant pure state. The forms of Vajrasattva and Yama with the pure realms and realms of being oscillate back and forth, one becoming the other, until the two interpenetrate completely and are seen to exist simultaneously. The shimmering pure white light and smoke-filled darkness remain distinct but inseparable. The lives of all tortured deluded beings and the manifestations of all the awakened state exist in just the same way.

This is the summit of the view.
This is the complete experience of wakefulness,
The inseparable unity of relative and absolute truth.

When Gesar sings this softly to his mother, Dzeden, as if recovering from a long fever, turns and looks at him. "I feel I have always known this. How did I forget?" Then Gesar sings again:

The completely awakened state,
Is self-purifying and self-expanding.

No world can hold it.
No lifetime can complete it.
No teaching can encompass it.
No memory can fulfill it.

Because it is pure, it is new:
It must always be re-discovered.

Because it expands
It arises constantly in momentary forms,
In transitions and in their qualities.

"But how can we who live and die find our way?" Dzeden asks. And once again, Gesar sings:

On the river of endless transition,
All beings move from realm to realm,
Creating and dissolving in them.

The Bardo of Existence moves in the duality
Of subject and object, being and realm.
Look in the mirror of Buddha Nature.
All inclusive, impartial and complete,
This is the living non-dual ground.

The Bardo of Dream moves in the duality
Of inner and outer phenomena.
Look in the mirror of luminosity.
All inclusive, impartial and complete,
This is the living non-duality of form and emptiness.

The Bardo of Meditation moves in duality
As a fabricated path between ignorance and wakefulness.
Look in the mirror of unfabricated Shamatha-Vipassana.
All inclusive, impartial and complete,
This is the living non-duality of thought and non-thought.

The Bardo of Dying moves in duality
As the conditions of duality collapse.
Look in the mirror of luminous empty Rigpa.
All inclusive, impartial, and complete,
This is the living non-duality of path and ground.

The Bardo of the Illusory Body and of Dharmata moves in duality
As the root of duality arises and wisdom dawns.
Look into the wisdom of the five wisdom lights.
All inclusive, impartial and complete,
This is the living non-duality of subject and object.

The Bardo of Becoming and of the Birthplace move in duality
As the unstable momentum of incomplete existence
Reaches the desire to solidify mind.
Look in the mirror of great compassion,
All inclusive, impartial and complete,
The living non-duality of prajna and upaya.

From this, there is no liberation.

Ground, path and fruition,
View, mediation, and action
Are inseparable.

Then Dzeden is exhausted, poised between waking and sleep. Slowly, like a wisp of smoke rising in a cloudless sky, a dream unfurls in her mind. She dreams that she is again a Naga princess happy in her father's palace deep beneath the sea. And suddenly she is alone. Then, as quickly, she finds herself on dry land. She gives birth to a child and all her longing for happiness pour out when she holds him. She walks through a desert. She watches a young man grow. She is again alone, and experiences unbearable pain in her body. She flies, she gallops, she starves, she burns in hell. She is carried upwards and she sees all the realms of being. Dzeden wakes from this torrent of hallucination with a scream. She is seated behind Gesar on Kyang Ko Kar Kar's back.

"Take me home," she sobs, "Please take me home." And so, without a word, Gesar nods and the miracle horse dives down to Dzeden's Naga palace deep beneath the sea.

*

Darkness in Ling

While Gesar, his mother and Kyang Ko Kar Kar voyage through the six realms, Gesar's bodily form remains on his bed in Ling, unconscious and barely breathing. His body is thinner, his breathing more labored, and his face darker. His hair and beard grow long and oily, and he smells of smoke. The expression on his face is tight and wrathful.

Summoned by the ministers of Ling, doctors from Tibet, India, China and Persia come and go. They examine Gesar carefully and take his pulses. Though unable to account for the King's condition, they formulate their theories and accordingly administer teas of rare herbs and precious minerals. They massage his limbs. They insert needles, and put cupping glasses and burning mugwort on his body. They fill the tent with the pungent scent of healing incense. Nothing they do has any effect.

Sechan Dugmo had been optimistic when the first Tibetan arrived with his black robes, his gold pointed hat, his ebony boxes and brocade bags. She was hopeful when the first Indian doctor came, shivering in his simple cotton clothes. She had been impressed by the first Chinese doctor in his long brocade coat and his long beard when he strode confidently into the tent. And the white-turbaned Persian with his short oiled beard and easy, joking manner, she even had hopes for him. But they accomplished nothing, and each left shaking his head and clinging to whatever dignity he could muster.

So she thinks bitterly that once again she is left behind while Gesar roams in realms she cannot imagine. She does not know where he is and what he is doing, and somehow she is expected to behave as if everything is normal when it is not. Her life seems like a dream of uncertain waiting, passed while Gesar goes off to do important and noble deeds. And now she feels like an automaton, as she dresses, cooks, and walks through the village with her head erect and projecting a kind of confidence she does not feel. What does Gesar expect of her, she wonders? Does he even think of her at all?

And the world around her feels empty, even false. Late spring has brought constant showers turning the earth to a sea of mud; drenching mists soak the black tents. Many great lords of Ling with those of their warriors who are so inclined continue to sit before King Gesar's tent waiting and praying. For them, she is almost invisible.

A great shrine has been set up beneath a lean-to on the muddy ground before the King's tent. Rows of silver offering bowls filled with incense, perfume and saffron water, oranges from Burma, pears from China, flowers from India, butter statues, and huge elaborate tormas are arranged before painted images of Buddhas, Bodhisattvas, Yidams, Protectors and of the Rigden Kings of Shambhala. Every day begins and every night ends with the echoing drone of horns, the wail of reeds, the clash of cymbals, and the rhythmic throb of drums. Throughout the four sessions of the day, Norbu Chopel in his finest robes sits at the head of the assembled ministers and people of Ling chanting invocations for Gesar's longevity. Day after day they perform liturgies to expel obstacles, and to ransom the King's spirit back from whatever invisible forces have taken him.

None of this means much to Sechan Dugmo, and none of it has any effect as far as she can tell. But they continue praying and importing doctors because it is the only thing they can think to do. Sechan Dugmo, though she sometimes joins them, thinks these efforts pointless. Over time, the great gathering at Gesar's tent has become a somber, even zombie-like succession of waiting, praying, and fatigue, as if wrapped in dense mist, everything has become suspended in a dream from which there is no escape or outcome.

Disturbing and obscure signs and omens intensify this atmosphere of strange unrest. Riders coming back from the plains report that spheres of red lightening shook behind banks of gray clouds. Herdsmen see snow lions dancing on snow peaks. Sudden shouts, as if from an approaching enemy army, wake people in the night. A hunter says he has seen Gesar ride across a distant mountain range. Farmers complain of winds that howl like abandoned children.

Sechan Dugmo sees how, like herself, people are becoming disheartened. She hears the rumors of strange portents, and she wonders where all this is leading. No one seems capable of taking the situation in hand. Norbu Chopel's earnest demeanor seems merely piety and his prayerful advice mere wishful thinking. The great General, Chopa Tongden's watchfulness seems simply paranoia, and his martial airs irrelevant. When Odkar Gyaltsen, Gesar's heir comes nervously to drink tea and sit at Gesar's side, she wonders what will become of the kingdom. And when the Princes of Hor and Jang make their infrequent calls, she is alarmed by their casual disrespect and transparent ambition.

Alone among these and the many other lords and ladies, Sechan Dugmo takes solace in the quiet simplicity of the Prime Minster, Tashang Denma. He comes to Gesar's tent late at night when all the others in the camp are asleep and she alone is sitting by her husband's unconscious form. He always acts as if he has merely dropped by, that Gesar is simply sleeping, and that nothing is happening out of the ordinary.

Then she can speak of her exhaustion and her fears. Denma just nods, and asks her to join him for a walk beneath the stars. One night, as they trek along the side of the rushing mountain stream up behind Gesar's tent, they hear a woman singing in a tent below.

Khye Ma
The hosts of bright stars are ours
As they shine down upon our land.
Shining down upon our land,
Leaping from the Big Dipper
The dragon of silver light hovers in the night.
Ah. Ah. The ancestor does not forget us.

From the black depth of the universe,
He glitters like the eyes of the sky.
He glitters like the eyes of the sky
And during the whole night,
He will watch over our house, our hearth, our friends.
Ah Ah. The ancestor does not forget.

When day breaks, the stars will fade.
The dragon's light will not be seen.
When the sun sets and he returns,
The dragon's light will then be seen
Leaping through the evening breeze,
The silent guardian of our rest.

Calling us onward
Each by name,
Ah. The ancestor does not forget us.

"It is difficult to feel very confident, but I know this," Denma says softly, as he sits beside Sechan Dugmo on a granite outcropping, "Whatever happens, we must not forget our kingdom. Hundreds of years from now, in times that will be filled with kinds of trouble we cannot even imagine, our whole life, the way we act will be a song people may still sing." And somehow, the Prime Minister's words comfort her.

Later that night, alone in his tent, Tsashang Denma sleeps deeply. He dreams he sees King Gesar sitting on a bearskin upon a golden throne supported by eight golden lions. Behind him, through a high window are glistening snow-capped mountains. The air around him is bright and cold and scented with juniper smoke. The atmosphere is clear and sharp. Hosts of warriors sit on his right; rows of beautiful women dressed in silk brocade sit on his left. An attendant stands before him holding a tablet with gold paper, and Gesar, concentrating fully, dips a brush into an onyx inkpot on a table by his side and turns to make a stroke. At that moment, although it is still dark, Tsashang Denma wakes and his heart is full of confidence.

In the following weeks, the rains of early spring subside, and the skies over Ling are turquoise blue. Pale green grasses sprout on the plains, and fill the air with their sweet scent. Birds return from the south and make their nests. Wildflowers bloom on the hill sides, tamarisks on the riverbanks turn pink. Horses and yaks in the pastures give birth.

It is at this time that a great caravan is seen ponderously making its way down from the high mountain pass towards Gesar's encampment. At last, it seems Lord Todong is making his appearance, and all are filled with apprehension. The splendid caravan with forty horsemen, as many servants and twice as many yaks decked out gaily in red and yellow ribbons and laden with heavy bales,then followed by carts and brightly painted carriages, files slowly into the encampment. Everyone gapes at this imposing retinue, but all are disconcerted when they find that it is not Todong himself, but Todong's son Nakchen Gyatso, his wife, the Shingti Princess, Methok Lhadze and their retinue.

Nakchen Gyatso is small and very dark with long black hair and a long mustache. His bloodshot eyes bulge, and he seem perpetually seething. He wears copper armor that glows as if it were red hot, and his helmet is surmounted with a raven's feather. He rides a tall, emaciated charger that has one white eye. He cannot keep his lip from curling as he looks down on the villagers around him. The people look so poor, their tents so shabby, their animals so unkempt. He cannot imagine why his father has coveted such a kingdom when everyone knows the world is filled with magnificent and complacent cities overflowing with every kind of wealth. And also, as all have heard, great armies may be forming in the North to conquer them.

The Shingti Princess, Methok Lhadze rides a milk-white palfrey and wears brocades of pale pink and blue embroidered with gold and silver flowers. Her face is round, her features delicate, and she smiles shyly at everyone as she rides by. She is pleased when even a little child smiles at her, and is touched by the many looks of admiration.

Odkar Gyaltsen, Gesar's heir, with all the ministers arrayed on either side, wait nervously in front of Gesar's tent to greet them.

"Cousin," Odkar Gyaltsen says mildly, "And most beloved Princess, thank you for coming here. I hope your journey was not difficult."

"Had Lord Todong or his family been notified of the great lord's condition, we would have been here sooner," Nakchen Gyatso replies coolly, but his wife gives him a warning glance and he continues in a more easy tone. "But at a time of such concern, the great Lord Todong, whose family held for so long the stewardship of Ling, sent us before him to offer such help as we can."

They enter Gesar's tent and make prostrations before his body. Sechan Dugmo notices that the pair looks at Gesar with a kind of curiosity that verges on avidity. And she likewise notices that even as they drank tea with her and exchange courtesies, neither looks her in the eye.

Courtesies accomplished, Todong's relatives and their entourage leave and busy themselves with setting up an elaborate encampment to the west of the main gathering. Soon they are giving banquets, giving presents, and making themselves agreeable to all and sundry.

Nakchen Gyatso has brought many impressive gifts: bolts of silk brocade for Sechan Dugmo; a large uncut ruby which seems to glow from within for Gesar's heir Odkar Gyaltsen; a precious sword of meteoric iron for the General Chopa Tongden; relics from Guru Rinpoche himself for Chopa Tongden, and for Tseshang Denma, ancient Chinese texts on rulership. To all the major nobles he gives similarly valuable and thoughtful presents and for the people as a whole, he provides barrels of rice wine when he gives great weekly feasts.

The Princes of Hor and Jang particularly like visiting with Nakchen Gyatso. They spend many hours hunting in the mountains and plains with him and many nights drinking his fine rice wine. Slowly, many of the young warriors, bored with inaction, tired of stories of long forgotten days and depressed by the gloomy atmosphere around Gesar's tent come to join them. They feel revived by the easy camaraderie of the new visitor and are stirred by his stories of conquests yet to come.

Daily, Nakchen Gyatso leads large hunting parties out onto the plains and up into the forests of the mountain lowlands. The warriors are happy at last to be riding across the plains and chasing one another through ravines and mountain valleys. Their hearts thrill to the pluck of the bowstring as they unleash arrow after arrow on their prey. Once again they feel awake and like true men.

Nakchen Gyatso laughs his wild laugh and sings as he races along:

My swift running horse is not so beautiful.
My swift running horse has a magic eye:
He sees through solid walls.
My swift running horse flies like a ghost:
None can escape when he has set his eye on him.

Every day Nakchen Gyatso brings back musk oxen, stags, does, fawns, pheasant, and ducks to feed the people of Ling. Thus, despite his occasional nastiness, many young men become his followers, and all except the most hide-bound of Gesar's old followers come to feel grateful for his presence in their midst.

Methok Lhadze also inspires an affectionate following. She invites all the young ladies and wives to tea parties and freely gives food and money to herdsmen's wives. But she spends most of her time visiting Gesar's wife. And indeed, Sechan Dugmo's impression of Methok Lhadze changes over the following weeks. When the Princess comes to Gesar's tent, she sits quietly and makes herself useful preparing tea, bringing towels and bowls of warm water and bringing food at mealtime. She always seems to know when Gesar's wife wants to be alone or wants to speak to some guest privately. She then discreetly withdraws. Over time, the two women begin to exchange small talk and later more personal confidences.

"Oh you know," the Shingti Princess whispers one evening, "When I was first married, I found my father-in-law crude and terrible. I was very unhappy and didn't see how I could live in the house of such a man.

"But really, over the years, he has taken his reverses to heart. He has even become something of a Buddhist practitioner. And truly, the change is quite amazing. His only wish now is to help those whom he once harmed."

"But even if that's the case, what could he possibly do?" asks Sechan Dugmo, to which the Princess only shrugs and smiles a sad and charming smile.

"Oh, I don't know." the young Princess artlessly prattles on: "I am only a visitor. It's not my place to say anything, but.... but well, it seems to me that all these doctors and all these ceremonies have not accomplished much. And perhaps for our ailing King, nothing can be done. But people are so sad and depressed, and for them something surely can be. It is spring. We could have a little fun, don't you think?" Sechan Dugmo sees that her new friend means well, and smiles. "Well maybe a little bit."

As time passes, when Tseshang Denma comes to call late at night, he often finds the two women chatting and giggling. At first when he visits, Methok Lhadze makes excuses and leaves, but after a while the Prime Minister comes to feel it is he who is intruding. Sechan Dugmo seems to have less and less to say to him, and so his visits become less frequent. And in truth, Sechan Dugmo feels a kind of guilty relief, for she is exhausted with futile depression and finds the cheerful banter of the little Princess a fresh breath of life.

Now it is only the ministers and the older citizens who continue to pray daily outside of Gesar's tent. By day the young men hunt and at night the air is again filled with the sounds of feasting and merriment, the laughter of young men and the flirtatious songs of young women.

Sechan Dugmo is glad to hear these sounds of happiness, but when she looks at the cold gaunt face of her husband, she feels unhappy and confused. "It is right for people to be happy. You should live or you should die." The words slip out of her mouth and she is appalled at herself. She looks guiltily at Methok Lhadze who gives a small smile but looks quickly away.

Also during the night, whispered rumors fly around the banquets and gossip crackles at the campfire. Some say that the Prime Minister has been the Sechan Dugmo's lover. Some believe she wants Gesar to die so she can marry the Prime Minister so she can found her own dynasty. Many wonder why the prayers of the people of Ling have no effect. All believe that Odkar Gyaltsen and all the ministers are weak. Some think that Gesar is already dead and it is kept secret so the old followers can continue to rule.

Sechan Dugmo does not hear these things, but feels eddies of lust, jealousy and disappointment swirl around her. And definitely she senses that she is no longer treated with the same respect as before.

*

Descending into the Naga realm
Now, Gesar and his mother together with the Miracle Horse Kyang Ko Kar Kar descend into the Naga realm, and come to the palace that was Dzeden's childhood home. There, accompanied by the soft mournful sounds of flutes and the slow beating of drums, Dzeden sings her last song.

The water around the palace that was once Dzeden's childhood home is now murky and filled with dark silt. No fish sparkle and dance nearby. The many surrounding beds of bright seashells have vanished. The palace is now a deserted roofless ruin, encrusted with contorted gray coral and overgrown with seaweed. Drifts of dirty sand cover the marble floors. There is no living thing to be seen or heard.

Gesar turns and looks at his mother. He is amazed and suddenly overcome. She has now returned to the form she had when she was a young Princess. Her face is smooth, pale and round as a pearl. Her hair is black and glossy, her limbs long and graceful. She wears a crown of reddish gold set with pale opals and wears a long gown of turquoise silk. Gesar stares at her, and somehow he knows that this is momentary: she is dying. He puts her down on a ruined bench beside a flight of broken steps and sits next to her. She smiles tenderly at him and sings:

My kind son,
Where I should take birth, I do not know.

I have dwelt in Hell for many lives.
In every realm, and even here, the home I longed for,
My pain and dying never stopped.
Now I see all realms as masks of Hell.

My son whom I longed for,
I have been a Preta many times.
Everywhere, even in this home I loved,
My cravings raged like an all-consuming fever.
Now I see all realms as versions of the Preta Realm.

My dear son, loyal and steadfast,
I do not know where I would live.

I lived the life of bird and beast.
But in every realm, even here where I was most happy,
I believed an instinct to survive would lead to happiness.
Now I see each realm as the dream or nightmare of an Animal.

My loving and compassionate son,
I was a human throughout many lives.
In every realm, even in this place, the home I had to leave,
My striving to know and act accordingly accomplished nothing.
I now see all realms as vain projections of the Human Realm.

My noble son, greatest of all warriors,
My strivings as an Asura lord were endless.
I do not know where I should take birth.

In every realm, even in the vanished splendor of this place,
My struggle to possess lasting bliss has never ended.
So I see all realms as unappeasable as the Asura Realm.

My sublime son, whose mind has never wavered,
My enjoyment as a God has filled the universe.
In every realm, even in this place which I have clung to,
I tried to escape and dwell in some perfect inner world.
My struggle to possess permanent bliss has never ended.
The Realm of the Gods is the delusion of every realm.

Oh my child, bright as the noonday sun,
Now I am dying,
And the elements of this sad life
Once again dissolve.

Once again I am afraid,
Afraid of dying,
Afraid of where I will be born again.

Gesar holds her, strokes her hair, weeps, and sings this song of parting:

Ah, Dzeden, my mother,
Through the trackless sky of naked awareness,
Moving on the pathways of love.
I have searched for you.

Venturing through the limits of my body and time,
Moving on the pathways of love,
I have penetrated the six realms within my own being,
And found you.

Moving on the paths of love,
I have cut through my past, present, and future
To rescue you from sorrow.
In every realm,
I have proclaimed the awakened state.

Now, in this moment when we are reunited,
We will separate again.
Though my mind does not waver,
Waves of sorrow engulf me.

Though in the empty sky of naked awareness
We do not separate,
Though in our hearts, love does not cease,
Life itself is marked by meeting and parting,
And we shall never see each other's face again.

Gesar and his mother hold each other and cry for a long time. Then Dzeden's mind begins to become cloudy and her body begins to shake. "Gesar, my beloved son," she wails," I am afraid. Please help me now." And Gesar speaks to her in a clear voice:

Now do not be afraid.
As the earth of your body collapses into water,
Your awareness is no longer limited

By the seeming solidity of experience.

As the water of your body dissolves into fire,
Your awareness is no longer dominated
By conceptual thought.

As the fire of your body evaporates into air,
Your awareness is no longer overpowered
By emotional dramas.

As the air of your body dissolves into consciousness,
All experience is hollowed out.
Everything about you is now changing beyond return.
There is no one grasping,
And nothing that can be grasped.

You see the dawn of empty luminous awareness:
It is your true nature
As space, as light, as duality,
It pervades all realms.
It can never be interrupted by birth or death
And never corrupted by any realm.
There is no longer anyone to be afraid,
Nor anything to fear.

Then slowly, Dzeden's mind loses contact with her body. Her body becomes cold, and her breathing labored. Finally, she takes her last breath. Her consciousness remains for a time within her body. Then Gesar performs a short liturgy for her:

First, he builds a shrine and places the seven offerings upon it before representations of Vajrasattva and of the Kingdom of Shambhala. Then he chants the refuge supplication and Bodhisattva vow, and invokes Vajrasattva. He supplicates the Buddhas of the past present and future, and calls on the Rigden Fathers. Then he chants this prayer called:

Song of The Sun of Confidence Bringing Liberation in the Innate Nature of the Heart.

OM VAJRASATTVA HUM
 KI KI KI
Now is the moment when death has come.

Now is the moment when the winds of time
Have dispersed the four great elements.

Now is the moment
When the illusion of individuality
Has been stripped completely away.
Pure naked awareness
Shines all pervasive in the dawn of Vajrasattva.

As he says the name of Vajrasattva, Gesar visualizes himself in that form.

Now Dzeden,
You are free from the painful limitations of self,
Free from the confusion of others.
You are free.
There is no you.

Empty awareness is your only mind.
All pervasive luminosity is your only speech
Unending love is your only body.
Everything you experience now
Is that.

SO SO SO

From within the heart of Vajrasattva
Unfolds vast, thousand petaled, pure white lotus
Whose center is a lake of liquid gold,
Whose tips vibrate blue, yellow, red and green.
It shines and fills the whole of space.

All that appears here as realm and bardo
Is the being of Vajrasattva.
This is primordial pure awareness.
This is complete luminosity.
This is the display of immeasurable compassion.

So, like a tiger bounding from shadow,
Like a lion leaping from a mountain peak,
Like a Garuda rising into empty space,

Like a Dragon unmoving in a swirling wind,
Dive into the golden lake.

As he says the word 'Dive', Gesar draws his mother's consciousness into his heart,
and lets it dissolve there.

KI KI KI
SO SO SO

In the heart center of the white lotus of all phenomena,
Shimmering amid the golden sea
Is the innate Kingdom of Shambhala.

Shambhala is an eight petalled lotus made of gold.
On its crystal anthers lies the capitol of Kalapa.
In the center of Kalapa is the Kalapa Court,
With crystal roof and gold pillars,
Lapis portals and ruby doors,
It is adorned with jeweled ropes, jade trees,
Silver bells, and sumptuous brocades.
It is wreathed in clouds of juniper, sage, and sandalwood incense.

Here the Rigden Kings sit on the eight lion throne.
Here the Rigden Queen presides from the antelope throne.
Here the father and mother lineages of warriors gather and sing.
This is the origin of all human dignity, gentleness, confidence and law.

Now Dzeden,
Fulfill your true nature,
Accept the treasury of all who are born or die in the human realm.
Enter the home of your heart,
The Kingdom of Shambhala.

Dive without fear into all-encompassing blackness;
Drown without hope in the heart blood of the Rigden Father's ink.
Confused and delirious in swirls of sensation,
Drink the amrita of the Rigden Father's deathless mind.
Blinded by sudden white light,
Be the stroke of the Rigden Father's crystal sword.
Lost in dreams of family and friends,

Sit in the golden court of the Rigden Father.
Overcome with doubt and longing,
Shout the imperial warrior's cry.

KI KI SO SO ASHE LHA GYEL LO
TAK SENG KHYUNG DRUK DI YAR KHYE.
SO SO SO

Completely melted
Completely dissolved
Inseparable from the warrior heart
Of the great Druk Sakyong,
Inseparable from the timeless lineage of warriors,
May all the love in every heart
Join as one in the innate Kingdom,
The eight-petaled golden lotus,
The Kingdom of the heart,
The Kingdom of Shambhala.

Whirling onward through all the illusions of space and time,
May we, as one Kingdom, blaze like the sun,
And beyond meeting and parting
Be a light to the world.

Then the entire visualization and its inhabitants dissolve into light. Gesar wraps his mother's body in a yellow silk cloth and places it across Kyang Ko Kar Kar's back. They rise through the ripples of the sea, and up into the clear soft air of evening. They fly higher and higher until they reach a grassy high mountain plain surrounded by deep pine forests and circled by bleak granite outcroppings. There Gesar gathers cedar wood for a funeral pyre and, as the sun sets and the early stars of evening glitter in the purple sky, he burns his mother's body. Throughout the night, and until all the embers of the fire were completely cold, Gesar sits and prays.

The next morning, when the sun has just risen, giving the granite peaks a pink hazy glow, Gesar sweeps his mother's ashes and places them in a vase. Horse and rider then fly out over the turbulent waters of the dark green sea, and Gesar scatters his ashes on the sparkling waves. To Gesar, it seems that the dark restless ocean is itself the moving form of the black Lord of Death, and in the lights shining on the rolling breakers, he sees the endless spinning of the six realms, wreathed in rising and descending sparks. So Gesar, sighs and sings:

The worlds of samsara
Are an endless song
Of joy and sorrow
Unfolding the wakefulness of space.
Space and awareness inseparable:
The six realms and the beings who prolong them,
The array of Pure Lands and Buddhas,
Samsara and nirvana,
The unbreakable continuum of birth and death,
The luminous path of the bardos
Is the spontaneous display of space
Awake.
Everlasting,
Indifferent to gain and loss.

Gesar is suddenly exhausted to the core. Kyang Ko Kar Kar's strength suddenly abandons him. All the power they roused in themselves to make their long journey through all the groundless hallucinations of existence falls away. Deep pervasive sadness weighs in their hearts.

Helplessly, the winds of karma carry them, and the longing of the people of Ling pull them back. Gesar is slowly drawn down into his body in the human realm.

PART 3
GESAR, THE UNWAVERING

In Ling it is the end of summer. Hot sun pours down the mountainsides like molten gold. Fields are deep green and melons and squash are ripe. Yet the vividness of the season only emphasizes the disquieting atmosphere in which so many of the people of Ling now live.

Everything feels unanchored. Peaches are sweet, green vegetables bright, the foals are lively, and children splash in the river amid the summer heat, but nothing seems quite real. Herdsmen used to long peaceful solitude in the high pastures find themselves restless. Merchants in their caravans pine for their homes. Craftsmen and weavers dream of distant cities. New lovers are anxious, and old lords seem merely to be going through the motions of rulership. Even those who spend their days in spiritual practice feel that their ceremonies, while sincere, somehow lack connection to anything. Like Gesar himself, the entire kingdom of Ling is suspended in a dreamlike realm between life and death.

At the end of this unsettled summer season, Lord Todong comes at last to Gesar's camp. He arrives in great state with a retinue of eighty warriors, three times as many attendants carrying flags and pennants, yaks, mules, carts and carriages. With them come ten monks blowing on long horns and shrill reeds attending an old lama swathed in brocade robes and carried on a small palanquin.

Todong himself rides a long-legged bay charger and wears gleaming bronze armor over maroon and white layman's robes. His head is newly shaven, and his helmet crowned with peacock plumes. He radiates confidence and splendor, and as he rides through the awe-struck crowds, he smiles benignly and bows from side to side. His regal bearing and the splendor of his equipage are magnetic.

But Nakchen Gyatso's eyes bulge and Methok Lhadze, laughing, covers her mouth. "Where did all those monks come from?" she whispers.

"He must have hired everybody from that decrepit monastery in the next valley. And look, there is his old pal, Kunga acting like some kind of monastery official. And look at that outfit. Stupendous. My father will succeed or die trying." He laughs aloud.

As Todong rides up to Gesar's tent, he sways slightly on his snow-leopard saddle and nods serenely. Todong's wife, Kurzar Sartok is wearing a fox fur robe, a gold brocade cap, and rides on a gray mare. Despite her opulence, she looks pinched and she glares at her husband and at all the warriors of Ling through whom they pass. The procession winds its way through the crowds astonished by such splendor. Despite the new popularity of his son, Todong himself is still not well liked, and his treacheries are well remembered. But his proud bearing and the magnificence of his large entourage are intimidating. So if some sneer remembering, others find themselves cheering.

Todong rides up to Gesar's tent between the rows of Lords who sit silently on either side. Then, without even dismounting, he declaims in a loud voice:

"Lords and Ladies, Warriors, Men and Women of Ling, you know me well. Because many of you have no love for me, I have considered carefully whether I should come or not. Thus I sent my beloved son and his precious bride.

"I have not ignored what has been happening here. Because I love our King, because I love our great and splendid land, I can stay away no longer.

"The great King Gesar is stricken with some strange disease. His condition neither worsens nor improves. As Gesar and his kingdom are one, the business of the kingdom must continue and prosper, if he is to recover.

"I stand in the ancient line of the kings of Ling. I am an emanation of Hayagriva the conqueror. No one has ever disputed this. My dreams are prophecies. No one has ever disputed this. In all the world, only Gesar is my equal, and only he has ever proved my better.

"Dreams sent by the gods have brought me here. I have not come to claim anything or to sow dissension. I have been enjoying a simple life, and only the needs of this kingdom would cause me to interrupt it. So I have come because I believe I might be useful. I have come here now to offer myself to you. I offer myself to each and every one to make use of as you may wish or need."

Todong dismounts and spends some time in Gesar's tent inspecting the body of the stricken King. He bends his head in prayer. He thanks Sechan Dugmo for all she has done and then he walks through the encampment accompanied by his son and daughter in law. His son introduces him to new friends, and he smiles and greets all who approach him.

Todong then leads his entourage to a broad meadow by the river a quarter mile to the west and there, next to his son, he sets up his own large encampment. At the center of his camp is a huge embroidered tent to serve as a monastery. To its right is a larger black wool tent for Todong, his wife and their attendants. Other tents house the warriors. A fence of wooden stakes with a great wooden gate and towers at the corners surround the entire camp.

In the following weeks, Todong establishes his routine. In the morning, he meditates with the monks. After lunch, he dresses in fine brocades and attends the ceremonies at Gesar's tent. He then walks through the encampment accompanied by his family or by his friend Kunga, visiting the markets and encouraging whoever he happens to meet. Afterwards he goes riding with his son, and in the evening he gives a feast. People begin to look forward to seeing him, and in his perambulations he is often asked for advice, for alms, and for his thoughts regarding small disputes that arise.

Indeed, after a while, many of Gesar's advisors come to visit and consult him. It appears to them that Todong is solely concerned with being helpful and no longer has any private ambitions. He encourages everyone to follow the ways Gesar has established, and is a steadying influence on the kingdom as a whole. But even if Todong gives no sign of being other than accommodating, a few of those who were closest to Gesar remained unconvinced. They are, however, reluctant to speak of their misgivings.

*

Beyond Misgivings and Deceit

Chopa Tongden, Gesar's old commander in chief, often rides alone high into the mountain passes. And as his horse strains upwards through the mountainous trail, he leans forward in his saddle and bursts out in a loud, furious voice:

**I am a scarred old man who has had a fortunate life
Because I have fought the best of battles:
And fighting for the best of rulers, I have always won.**

**I am a scarred old man who has had a fortunate life
And cannot forever be hidden in the dark.**

**But when the true lord returns to rule in Ling,
This scarred old man will fall on the usurpers
Like an ancient meteor dropping from the midnight sky.**

Gesar's spiritual advisor, Norbu Chopel returns to his retreat place in the north. Late in the night, as he looks at distant snow-capped peaks glittering beneath the stars and smells the snow carried on a soft breeze, he sings:

**The human realm is treacherous and tricky,
But here on peaks that touch the sky,**

There is no deceit.
Oh may the prayers of a sincere heart
Open all eyes to see it.

Gesar's Prime Minister, Tsashing Denma finds that he has little to do since Todong's overseers manage day-to-day affairs. The harvest that year is a good one, and all the foals and yak calves born in the spring grow fat and strong. Trade increases and with it the prosperity of the people of Ling. Everyone, once again, is very busy. Except for Tseshang Denma, few now wait and pray outside Gesar's tent, or make offerings at the shrine that still remained there. He is content to read, meditate and to wait.

Gesar's breathing is less labored, but it seems to Sechan Dugmo that he is becoming a different being. He is emaciated and his skin is now almost bronze, as if he were becoming the statue of some ancient war god. He now has a long black beard, long black hair, bushy eyebrows and an expression at once sad and implacable.

"He is better, don't you think?" Methok Lhadze asks Sechan Dugmo early one morning, and Gesar's wife allows that it might be true. "And it's just as I said about Lord Todong too. Isn't that right?" But here, Sechan Dugmo becomes suspicious though she can find no outward reason for being so.

Far off on a hillside, in a dark valley in a pine forest above a trickling stream, Gesar's heir Odkar Gyaltsen dreams of Gesar. The Lion Lord is seated on his Horse of Wind, Kyang Ko Kar is whirling through the sky as through a thundercloud. Left and right and all about he slashes the air, and the arc of his sword blade emits bolts of lightning. Although the Lord fights furiously, and the thunder that follows his sword is filled with shrieks and roars, no enemy can be seen. Odkar Gyaltsen wakes, feeling suddenly cold and very alone, and he sings these words:

Oh, how do I serve a Lord who never relents
Even if now he is only in my heart?

*

Beyond Life and Death
As late fall descends, Ling is bathed in the pale copper light of a mild and bountiful autumn. The harvests, the most plentiful that anyone can remember, have been taken in. Merchants return from their long journeys to the North and South with great quantities of gold, silver, brocade and tea. Herdsmen come down from the mountain summer pastures with ever-larger numbers of young horses, yaks and dri.

Todong is increasingly at ease in his role as lord of Ling and feels that finally he is living the life that always should have been his. The ministers of Ling now hold their councils in his tent and look to him for leadership and guidance. Where formerly

Todong arbitrated disputes informally, now he holds court three times a week, and his daily walks among the people become almost a formal procession. Emissaries from some of the neighboring nations have begun to arrive, bearing lavish gifts and treating Lord Todong as the ruler of Ling. All this is as Todong had hoped and planned for, and it seems to have happened quite naturally. So with the exception of those who were most loyal to Gesar, the people of Ling begin to feel relieved as prosperity and ease return to their lives. Their recent misgivings have faded. The challenges of spiritual practice and the rigors of martial arts now seem unnecessary.

In this optimistic atmosphere, the existence of Gesar himself is a cause of awkwardness, and it seems in many ways best simply to ignore the situation. Todong's visits to pray beside his stricken kinsmen become less frequent and are usually very brief. Amid the press of business, most find it difficult to put aside time to attend the prayers offered daily for Gesar. When Gesar's name is mentioned, people feel a tremor of guilt and unease. Certainly no one wishes the great lord to be dead, but increasingly it is obvious that he has no function among the living. Even Sechan Dugmo, alone late at night in her tent, as she listens to the echo of young people laughing around a fire somewhere far off, has to acknowledge to herself that she no longer believes that Gesar will ever recover.

The most loyal of Gesar's ministers and those who still attend King Gesar cannot ignore this. So, though happy for the prosperity of the people, they fall prey to bitterness and sorrow. Their distress is a reminder to all who see them, and creates a kind of faint unpleasant odor amid the general happiness.

"Gesar, Gesar, Gesar," cries Nakchen Gyatso, Todong's son, "Look at the long faces of his old cronies. Ungrateful for all you do, they pine for their so-called good old days. And what were those good old days? Gesar was rarely here, and his people were left to a lonely existence, scrounging twigs and branches for firewood to cook their crude and meager meals.

"But try to mention that. Try to point out to those old buffoons what things are really like now, and you get a mournful head waggle and windy sighs. And you can't tell them that Gesar is dead, even though he might as well be."

Then late one night, surrounded by his ministers, eating and drinking someone happens to mention Gesar's name. Lord Todong is suddenly enraged. He makes up his mind, and smashes his great fist on the table.

"Enough." he roars. "I will no longer be a prisoner of the past!" And then he pulls himself together and continues in a more reasonable tone. "No one denies Gesar's greatness. But the time has come to acknowledge the fact that he is not just in a trance or a slumber from which he will rise, but that he is dead and maintains the outer illusion of life for who knows what reason. His time is over."

Then Todong and his entourage talk late into the night, devising the best way for bringing the beloved Gesar to his final rest. They must find a way to do so without risking the loss of their present happiness, but they reach no conclusion.

That night Todong cannot sleep as thoughts roil in his head. It is only as the sky begins to lighten that he falls into a deep sleep, and has a dream so vivid and real that when his servants come to wake him, he is for some time unsure of where he is. Immediately he calls his family and close friends around him, and, still sitting in his bed, tells them what he has just experienced.

"Last night, I could not sleep. My thoughts raced everywhere until suddenly it seemed that my body was made of lead and pressed down upon me like a mountain. Whether I opened or closed my eyes, all kinds of dreams and mirages moved across my gaze.

"Thirst overcame me and my mouth was dry. I couldn't hear anything but my own thoughts, and it seemed like smoke was swirling all around me. I felt feverish and thought I was burning up. I couldn't remember my own name and it seemed like fireflies were sparkling everywhere. Then there was a roaring of winds that deafened me. All the world seemed to flicker as if it were a light about to be blown out. The noise was unbearable, and somehow, all at once I fell asleep.

"For some time I lingered in a dark place of which I have no memory, but slowly as the light around me became stronger, I saw Gesar the Lion Lord as clearly as I see you now. He was wearing his full armor and glowed with purpose and energy. And as I floated back from him, I could see that he was hovering within the great black body of Yama, the King of death. Within Yama's body he was moving up and down on a highway of light, riding on his wonder horse, Kyang Ko Kar Kar. And clasped in his arms, was his mother, the Naga Princess Dzeden. As he passed near me, he looked at me and smiled...tenderly."

"I was so shocked that I immediately awoke. The true and unhappy meaning of this vision is all too clear."

Though Todong's wife, as always, wonders if he is simply making this up, she can see how he could make use of it. But everyone else is deeply moved by the evident surprise and sincerity in Todong's voice. Then he continues in a thoughtful tone.

"My friends, as you know, the beautiful Dzeden died many many years ago. Gesar is with her now in the domain of the lord of death. None of you can doubt what this means. Even though his body may be warm and a feather of breath still may pass his lips, King Gesar is dead."

Then gravely he instructs them that in order to prepare for what is to come, each person there should tell of his dream to two others and no more. In this way the shock will ripple slowly and not cause any upheaval. He sends them all out, but sends Kunga to ask the Abbot to consult his astrological calendars to determine the best day for a funeral. "And make sure he doesn't hit on some date too far off," Todong hisses at his friend's departing back. Kunga cringes to hear this.

Sechan Dugmo has heard the rumors, and knows immediately they are true. She feels trapped as if a windstorm has come up behind her while she is walking over a mountain pass, making it impossible for her to stop, return or to go in any direction but one.

She hoped always that a time would come when Gesar was no longer off at war and they would live at last in peace. She hoped their kingdom would finally be harmonious and content. But time and events are now carrying Gesar away from her. Perhaps he has left already, and his vision for an enlightened society gone with him. But she cannot envision living in this world without him even if after days and nights tending him, her hope has dwindled. She is exhausted, unable to think, and swamped in a lassitude of resignation.

Accordingly, two days later, early on a crisp cold autumn morning when the air is filled with the smell of mountain snow, she watches in tired indifference as Todong's son, Nagchen Gyaltsen, wearing a robe of black silk embroidered with thunderbolts rides on down the valley of Ling at the head of a great procession. Behind him, on a saffron palanquin comes the abbot of Todong's monastery dressed maroon robes, a gold brocade vest and wearing a high yellow hat. He is followed by an assemblage of distinguished scholars, attendants and monks blowing horns and perfuming the air with clouds of sandalwood incense. They, in turn, are followed by a crew of workmen and three large carts pulled by yaks. As they move slowly towards Gesar's tent, the monks chant in deep voices, and a growing crowd gathers to see what is happening.

As she watches the crowd winding its way towards her, she feels only deepening sadness. Methok Lhadze who has been her constant companion senses her mood. "Oh, please don't be upset." But Sechan Dugmo withdraws back into her tent to change into her formal red robe, and prepare tea for her unwanted guests.

Soon enough, Nagchen Gyaltsen and his procession arrive. He dismounts and waits for Sechan Dugmo to emerge. When she does, he bows low to her, and declaims in a stiff formal voice:

"Sechan Dugmo, peerless and most faithful consort, great Queen of Ling, we arrive this morning on a sad but crucial mission. From ancient times, tales have been told of great beings whose valor and compassion was so great and whose meditation was so powerful that their consciousness remained in their bodies for the benefit of all who lived. Though they were dead, their bodies remained unmoving and uncorrupted.

"But it is also part of ancient lore, that there comes a time when this meditation must be ended, and these great heroes freed from the prison of their exhausted bodies to venture on and help other beings elsewhere.

"Lord Todong, emanation of Hayagriva and justly renowned in prophecy, has been sent a vision. He has had it written down so that at leisure you may inspect it. But what has been revealed is that, sadly madam, your lord and the master of us all, Gesar King of Ling and master of the four kinds of warriorship now journeys in the land of death. Thus, his journey amongst us is now ended.

"Accordingly, Lord Todong burdened with his responsibilities to this kingdom, and his heart heavy with this sad obligation, has consulted his astrologers to know has if the time had come when great King Gesar's great blessings are called for in some other realm.

"All indications, charts, and divinations come to one point: this precious form of Gesar, King of Ling must be dissolved before the first snow falls. All agree that, should the present form linger into wintertime, hardship and misfortune would befall this land.

"There can be no doubt, and this must cause you greatest grief, that now we all must bid farewell to our valorous king. He has exhausted himself in the service of his people and has earned his freedom and his final rest. And hard as this must be for all who are so loyal and devoted, I give you now the account of Lord Todong's vision and decree."

And with that, Nagchen Gyaltsen pulls from his robe a leather wallet stuffed with papers, and bowing, hands them to Sechan Dugmo. She takes them and, because she is so completely stunned and does not know what else to do, tries to read them. But the words blur before her eyes. She can think of no way to refute or forestall this death sentence. She barely notices when Nagchen Gyaltsen takes back the papers and barely hears as he reads them to the people in his loudest voice:

"It shall be that the exhausted and hollow form of King Gesar, the Lion Lord of Ling shall be removed from this tent, and conveyed to a nearby ceremonial tent which shall be set up now. There his body will be placed for the last time upon his throne. He shall remain there for seven days while all who wish to receive his final blessings may see him. Prayers for him shall be uninterrupted. Then in a great pyre of sandalwood and cedar, his body shall be burned, and all appropriate ceremonies will speed him on his way.

"Lord Todong now proclaims that even if the Lion Lord, Gesar, King of Ling is no longer with us in body, he shall remain forever in our hearts. And so that he remain forever a living presence for all human kind, Lord Todong at his own expense will commission the greatest Lamas in Tibet to compose invocations and sadhanas which will performed continuously at a shrine which Lord Todong will soon build here. Thus may the end of his earthly life begin his unending presence in the world."

The crowd falls still, and it seems to Sechan Dugmo that even the birds, and the winds and the nearby stream make no sound. The sun and the sky become dark and the earth unstable. Sechan Dugmo faints.

*

Calling on the Great Protectress, Ekajati
While these events swirl around outside him, King Gesar lies comatose in his tent. He knows where he is, but his homeland now seems merely one of many dreams

flickering amid visions of other realms, memories of his mother, her sufferings and her death. But slowly, as if moving forward through a fog, all that has happened in Ling while he's lain stricken is becoming clear. He sees what Todong and his people plan for him. The devotion of those close to him touches his heart, but their feebleness is dispiriting. His people's fickle doubts oppress him. Their persistent neediness and wanting have weakened whatever they had ever learned in their time with him. Since things are now going well, they have no need of someone such as he. And just by still existing, he reminds them of possibilities they have seen within themselves, of a heroism that is now inconvenient. Now they will be only too happy to see him gone. Gesar's sorrow makes it impossible to speak or move his limbs. He is engulfed by depression, and so, to dispel his dark mood, he calls on the great protectress Ekajati.

This is accompanied by cymbals that make a low growling sound.

AH BHYO
In the raging torrent of life
Where wisdom cannot separate from ignorance,
Nor birth from death, hot from cold,
Nor joy from grief, nor light from darkness
Stillness from movement, courage from fear,
Silence from sound;

In this unending torrent of life
Which is a boiling ocean of living blood,
Spontaneously, you arise.

Ekajati, Ekajati,
You arise in chaos
And do not move from there.
Ancient and immense,
Your body is blue like the midnight sky.
Your single lock of turquoise hair
Whirls and slices.
Nothing escapes the light
Of the single eye in the center of your forehead.
Nothing escapes the rending
Of your single white razor fang.
Nothing is not nourished
By the single breast in the center of your chest.
You hold a living human heart in your right hand

And an army of all-consuming jackals in your left.
Your furious retinue fills the air with screams
And the sky with stars.

Queen of Mantra,
You are the secret of the awakened state;
Queen of Drala,
You are the phenomena of the awakened state;
Queen of Riches
You are the uninterrupted experience of the awakened state.

Self-existing being,
The fourth without the third,
You turn the three mandalas
Of body, speech and mind
Inside out.

Unchanging and implacable
You are the single mind of enlightenment.
And your shattering cry calls us out.

Ekajati, Ekajati
Accept me now and hold me close.
AH BHYO SARVA SAMAYA HUM

Having offered this prayer, Gesar feels that he is rising lightly into the sky. He sees his body lying below him. He sees the encampment around his black tent. He sees Dzeden, his heir, his general, his heir; he watches Todong and his family holding court. But as he looks toward the horizon, he is drawn to a far off snow-peak brighter than the rest. A kind of power there attracts him. His spirit feels light, and effortlessly he moves towards it.

PART 4
ENTERING THE KINGDOM OF THE HEART

Now, to the accompaniment of chimes, drums, and deep gongs playing in undulant sounds, Gesar slowly returns to life in Ling as he dreams of life in the Kingdom of Shambhala.

It is said that travelers moving through the desolate wastes between the mountains of Tibet and China have, on occasion, happened to approach the borders of the Kingdom of Shambhala. And they have, depending on their intentions, experienced it in different ways. To those in search of gain but not seeking Shambhala, it has appeared as an unaccountable sudden fear and sense of foreboding. To kindly people, traveling but not looking for Shambhala, it seemed like a sudden inspiration, like a word on the tip of their tongue or like a remembered happiness they cannot quite grasp. To enemies and spies who have heard of Shambhala and are seeking to find ways to conquer or suborn it, or to merchants looking merely to make a profit, the kingdom appeared as a vast, impassable and overwhelming ring of white mountains reaching to the sky and covered with snow and ice. To philosophers or spiritual seekers looking to enter Shambhala, the mountains appeared as an elusive barrier of concepts and confused emotions within their minds. Thus they saw only a shimmering mirage.

But Gesar now finds himself riding above Shambhala on the back of his miracle horse, Kyang Ko Kar Kar. As if carried on a gentle spring breeze, horse and rider fly easily above the ice walls of its mountains. Within the protection of this towering circular ice wall, the Kingdom of Shambhala lies before them, broad and spacious, its terrain varied and accommodating. For this reason it has always been known as the "Kingdom Held by the Source of Happiness". It is shaped like a fully open eight-petaled lotus, with eight lesser kingdoms divided one from the other by broad rivers.

In the center of the kingdom, like the anthers of a lotus, is a high plateau. There, Kalapa, the capitol of Shambhala known also as "Great Renown", rests like a jeweled crown with its central palace glowing amid the gardens of Malaya and their sparkling lakes and fountains. This is the seat of the Rigden kings, holders of the Vajra Caste, and the rulers of Shambhala. The twenty-five lords of Kalapa exist all at once outside of time and manifest one by one within it. Their minds pervade the Kingdom of Shambhala as the sun in all its cycles.

All who dwell in Shambhala move through birth, old age, sickness and death. But here, these are taken not as misfortunes but as the seasons are experienced in other realms. The entire journey of living and dying is realized as the unfolding display of wakefulness. Thus the people of Shambhala, no matter what their station, take pride in their way of life, in their families, loved ones, livelihood, clan, and ruler. Their lives are dignified and they uphold the highest standards of the warrior path. They celebrate their traditions by maintaining strong armies, engaging in great skirmishes, by observing the rites of the worldly and transcendent deities, by singing, dancing, calligraphy and poetry, and by feasting. The manner in which they do so varies in each of Shambhala's four principal kingdoms.

The Eastern Kingdom

In the East is the kingdom called "The Proud". This is a hot land consisting of vast alluvial plains, dense jungles and deserts. The people here are dark-skinned and tend towards corpulence as they age. Most farm and live very simply. Women are venerated; they uphold a separate way of life from men and rarely exert political power. There are however numerous cities in which life is extremely opulent. Here are many artisans, jewelers, metalworkers, potters, and most famously, weavers. The army is especially famed for its battle elephants and engines of war. The court attracts many artists and fosters the development of elaborate music, poetry, dance, ornate architecture and painting. The court is especially renowned for the complex presentations of epic theater that lasts for many days. The food here is complex and very spicy and the perfumes dense and rich.

Many philosophers and sages were born in this kingdom. Spiritual practice here is famed for its devotional quality, and the citizens in general are known for the sincerity of their moral conduct. Here the sutras are upheld with special care; the Buddha's disciples, Ananda and Shariputra are venerated. Extensive offerings are made to the worldly deities with special attention to the thirty-three gods.

The ruler here is called "The Great Tiger Treasury of Mercy" and, by the power of compassion, he manifests in many times and places, but in the outer human realm and time he is most famous as Ashoka Maharaja.

The Southern Kingdom

The Southern Kingdom is called "The Vast Field". All four seasons here are intense, and the terrain is very mountainous, dotted with sparkling lakes and broad streams.

The people are short, wiry, and rather pale. Women manage their households, become famous as artists and warriors and occasionally rule. Farmers dwell in small villages on the plains, but most of the populace lives in cities where the mountain valleys meet.

Most city dwellers are involved in manufacturing and trade, and their products are famous throughout Shambhala for superb workmanship and design. Porcelain, mechanical devices, silk brocade, and many other innovations of great technical ingenuity pour from their factories. The army is feared for its ferocious discipline, and its warriors uphold the highest standard of martial arts. The court is famous for its blend of austere simplicity and great elegance. All the arts it fosters have those characteristics. Particularly celebrated is the puppet theater in which three puppeteers manipulate large dolls in an amazingly lifelike way. The food is simple and its manner of presentation very refined. Perfumes are subtle and flowery.

There are many great scientists and engineers here. Spiritual practice is known for its harsh discipline and single mindedness, and these qualities pervade the manner of the populace as well. Here the outer tantras are also upheld, and Avalokiteshvara is revered. Of worldly deities, offerings are made principally to the Nyen deities.

The ruler of the Southern Kingdom is called "The Great Dragon Apex of Confidence". By his compassion, he manifests his inner nature in many times and realms, but he is known in the outer human realm and time as Prince Shotoku Taishi.

The Western Kingdom
The name of the Western Kingdom is "The Flexible". Its terrain consists of great empty deserts to the North and West, vast tracts of farms irrigated by rivers in the center, and temperate coastal land bordered by ocean-like inland seas. This is the most populous of all the eight kingdoms of Shambhala and accordingly the most diverse. Some people here are very tall, some short, some thin some heavy, some dark and some pale. Women are enormously powerful here and influential in all aspects of life. They are frequently rulers. But here also most of the people engage in farming, and they are famed for their filial piety and loyalty to their families. All manner of goods and handicrafts are made in the cities and provide good cheap simple necessities as well as the most elaborate luxuries.

The army is known for its strategic acuity and complex military formations as well as for its sheer size. Many styles of art, writing, music, drama, and architecture are encouraged and all are represented in the vast palaces of the court. The life of the court is renowned for its bureaucratic exactitude and painstaking codification of all that is of concern to the citizenry. It is also known for the ceremonial precision with which it carries out its functions. The food is considered the most complex, diverse, and delicious in the whole world. Its perfumes are too numerous to characterize in a phrase or two.

Many great doctors, geomancers, astrologers, poets and famous jurists and theorists of statecraft were born here and attained great influence. Its spiritual practitioners are known for their scholarship as well as their willingness to withdraw from the world. The practices of the Mahamudra are maintained perfectly, particularly those, which can be practiced in the context of secular life. Manjusri is cherished, and among worldly deities, offerings were made especially to those of the Lu domain.

The lord of the Western Kingdom is "The Great Garuda of Luminosity".

His inner nature is displayed in many realms and times but is famed in the outer human realm and time as the Yong Le Emperor, Chu Ti.

The Northern Kingdom

The Northern Kingdom is called "The Joyous". Its land is almost completely covered with harsh, jagged, impassable mountains, but there are some broad valleys, lakes and torrential rivers between the endless snow-capped ranges.

Pine forests cover the lower slopes, and so timber is plentiful although it could not be transported far. The weather here is very cold, and, other than winter, all the seasons are brief. This kingdom is very sparsely populated and very poor in material advantages. The people are small, thick-bodied, and dark from sunburn. Women here are very strong, but almost never rule. Some are farmers, but most of the people lead a nomadic life of herdsmen moving from valleys in the winter to higher pastures in the spring and summer. The people of this kingdom are famous throughout Shambhala for their toughness and determination as well as their independence and resourcefulness. There are some handicrafts of a rather primitive nature, but religious painting and sculpture are highly evolved. The army is small and admired for its guerrilla tactics and the ferocity and courage of its individual soldiers. Small towns coalesce around the courts of the lesser nobility and the only city large is clustered around the king and his court. Rugged martial simplicity, intense spiritual practice, and raucous feasts mark the life in this court. Epics of the great warriors, poems of realization, riddles and long historical poems are chanted and sometimes danced during these feasts. The food is considered by outsiders to be very poor, and there are no perfumes.

Great as it is, the fame of the warriors here is overshadowed by the renown and awe accorded the spiritual practitioners of the Northern Kingdom. The intensity with which the many men and women who practice in caves and the single-minded way they combine, study, meditation and devotion produced generations of multitudes of yogi- scholars with great powers of siddhi. They are sought out through the whole of Shambhala. The inner tantras are maintained in unbroken lineages of great antiquity. Vajrapani is especially revered and offerings are made to the worldly deities of the Lha domain.

The ruler of the Northern Kingdom is Sengchen Norbu Dradul, "The Great Lion Jewel Who Overcomes All Demons". Through limitless compassion, he manifests his inner nature in countless realms and times and has appeared in the outer human realm and time as Gesar, King of Ling.

As Gesar and Kyang Ko Kar Kar pass over this northern kingdom, the noble steed whinnies exultantly. Joy blazes in Gesar's heart. He wants nothing more than to meet the rulers of this land. The Miracle Horse pulls down on the reins in his haste to descend into Shambhala, and they fly towards Kalapa like a shooting star in a cloudless mid-day sky.

*

The dream of this great realm begins to fade, and once again Gesar finds himself lying immobile in his tent. He watches unmoving over the next two days, as crowds of nomads, farmers together with their families, pilgrims and mendicants, and caravans of nobles fill the roads and pathways to Ling like streams in spate. None can quite believe that the great King of Ling is now dead, and all are anxious to look on Gesar's face for one last time.

Gesar's Prime Minister, Tsashang Denma, his general, Chopa Tongden, his spiritual advisor, Norbu Chopel, and his heir, Odkar Gyaltsan together with Gesar's old guard also gather. Although Todong has offered to provide them with lavish accommodations, they prefer to establish a little camp in the foothills apart from the general crowd. They are however carefully watched. Even if they only go to the services in the tent and have occasional meetings with Sechan Dugmo, Todong still wishes to be certain that they make no effort to organize any kind of opposition to his plan. But it seems the long wait during Gesar's illness has broken them, and they now have nothing left.

All the land around Gesar's tent is filled with the encampments of visitors. Lines of people waiting to bid farewell to the famous warrior circle the tent where he is seated in state. Some people pray as they wait, others laugh nervously and gossip with friends they have not seen for years. Vendors of drinks, noodles, fried bread, as well as curios and souvenirs set up stalls to accommodate the visitors, and the assemblage begins to feel something like a carnival.

Within the funeral tent however, the atmosphere is thick with grief. Ceremonies now have a desperate fervor. But through the heavy scent of incense, there is no denying that the odor of putrefaction is becoming stronger. Gesar's body is shrinking. becoming dark as a smoked haunch of meat. Thus even the most skeptical now believe that he is indeed dead. Sechan Dugmo feels herself borne helplessly towards Gesar's impending cremation as if carried on a rushing stream to an abyss.

On noon of the second day, when the lines around the tent are longest and the surrounding crowds thickest, there is a stir when an old woman riding on a donkey presses her way up to the tent where Gesar sits. She is scrawny, very tall and dark with a bluish cast and her donkey is jade colored. She smells strongly of burnt bone.

Her expression is wild and furious; her red-rimmed, bloodshot eyes glare at everyone she passes. Because of the stench and her expression, the crowd draws back to let her pass.

She is dressed in heavy black robes covered with ash and her long white hair swirls in the wind. Indifferent to the crowd around her, knocking people this way and that, cursing and spitting, she rides up to the tent door where there is a little clearing. Suddenly people stop their talking, praying, eating and selling, and all fall still.

She stands up on the donkey's back perching like a crow, and towering over the crowd, she brandishes an ancient dog-eared text at them. Then she leers, displaying a mouthful of black and broken teeth, and in a voice like a vulture's screech, begins her harangue.

"Vile. Disgraceful. A great warrior fights for you his entire life. He shows you how to live. Now when you feel you have a nice comfortable life, you race to burn him up.

"You are so impatient to enjoy yourselves that you cannot even do it properly. Your new ruler, this Todong about whom everyone knows, wallows in comfort and sanctity and dreams. He consults the silent stars and texts which only charlatans ever claimed to understand. And he decides that the passing of this precious hero should be celebrated at a convenient time.

"Has he consulted our age old traditions here? No. Has he talked to anyone who has seen the stars through the eyes of the first Buddha, the glorious Kalachakra? No."

The crowd is mesmerized and appalled. The old crone seems to swell before their very eyes like an approaching monsoon. Her eyes glitter like sparks of lightning, and her rage is deafening.

"If any of your so-called lamas could add accurately and if any of them had any knowledge of the Kalachakra Tantra or of the commentaries by the Imperial Rigdens Manjusri Yaksas or his son Pundarika, it would, I assure you, be very clear that you have not planned the cremation of your beloved lord for the correct date or time. And if your leaders can make mistakes like that, what other great errors they are making? Why is such a grave and irrevocable undertaking entered into so rashly?

"If some scholar among you can actually read, here is a real prophecy: this path you are on will bring your land to ruin. Hordes of barbarians will build latrines on your graves. Your children will be sent to the four directions. Within two generations, they will not even know your language any more.

"Perhaps you have your own reasons for doing what you do. I don't want to know them. I couldn't care less. I have said what I've said only out of respect for the great compassion that the unequaled warrior and Lion Lord of Ling extended to you. Looking at your greedy, craven, gawking faces, I have no idea what he saw in you."

And with that, the old crone begins to shimmer like a mirage of blue-black smoke. Soon she is almost completely transparent and within seconds she is gone.

When Sechan Dugmo is told of the strange crone's speech and prophecy, she feels a glimmer of hope. She is sure that somehow this is Gesar's doing, and she smiles. Methok Lhadze is with her when she hears and finds the Queen's reaction somewhat odd.

"But Mistress? This is a prophecy of misfortune."

"Oh," Sechan Dugmo replies, "It is just that in such a time of sorrow, any postponement of the final parting with my lord gives me hope." But Methok Lhadze is suspicious and quickly goes to tell Lord Todong what has happened.

"She thinks that Gesar conjured up this apparition, and that he is now moving to unseat you, as he has done before. I know her well, and believe me this is what she thinks."

"Bah," snarls Todong who, resting in his tent after the noon meal, is angry at this obstacle to the smooth accomplishment of his plans. "What that woman thinks is not important any more. What is important is that at this moment the people must not lose faith in me." And with that he dismisses his daughter-in-law and summons his crony Kunga who arrived almost immediately.

Todong chuckles when he sees his old drinking partner decked out in monastic robes. "You know, old friend, I still cannot get used to seeing you dressed that way."

"Well, I am not quite used to seeing you looking so regal either." Todong seems displeased by this casual remark, and so Kunga moves on quickly. " But my lord, as you well know, I was indeed a monk for many years. And when you asked me to play that role again, I was sure that I could be as good an impostor as any. So I did my best to act in accord with all the monastic rules and requirements.

"Now I find, much to my surprise, that the role truly suits me. I like listening to the old abbot's discourses. I like studying and practicing with the other monks. And whether it's age or wisdom, I feel at home living a monastic life. In fact, strange to say, it feels quite genuine." Todong looks at his friend doubtfully, but then smiles.

"Well, I have certainly heard of stranger things, and, under the circumstances, perhaps it will be to our advantage." And he goes on to tell his friend about the crone and her pronouncements.

"Oh my, this is not exactly an ordinary problem, is it? How can I help you?" asks Kunga.

"I think..." Todong strokes his beard, and gives his friend a sly look. " It might be best, seeing how there is such an uproar, and seeing how people, for some reason, find this strange being and her outrageous claims credible; it might be best to make a certain accommodation."

"But perhaps this is just a demoness stirring up trouble."

"Well, then she has succeeded, and I, for one, am not about to debate the point. I want you to ask the abbot to say that he has reviewed the work of his scholars and has found a very small error. This error was a miscalculation of a mere two days, and the cremation of the Lion Lord will be postponed by exactly that time. He must assure people that there will be no further error and the demoness will not return."

Kunga is dismayed, and replies angrily. "The abbot is a man of learning and upright virtue. He should not be demeaned and compelled to act for your political convenience."

With that, Todong begins to shriek: "I made you into the monk you are so happy now to be. I made that impoverished priest into a grand abbot with fine brocade. You are both very good at accepting lavish donations. Now I expect you to play your part.

"I want this trouble to end, and if your abbot needs justification, explain that his proclamation is to sustain the devotion and well being of my subjects here and now." Then, in a furious voice, he sings this song:

It is pleasant to dwell in meditation
While confusion threatens the lives of ordinary folk.
It is pleasant to discourse on emptiness
When children must be fed
And old people need to be kept warm.

The needs of humans are endless but simple.
The path of the ruler is the comfort of his people.
He rises on their security and falls by their doubt.
And leaderless,
Humans are like a dispersed herd
Running in the dark from the sharp teeth of wolves.
Whether or not I am a good and just man,
I will save them from this fate.

Kunga looks unhappily at his old friend and patron; "I thank you for your many years of kindness to me, but we have both changed. You have always envied Gesar, and now you are on the verge of assuming his seat. I too am closer to something I have always wanted. But I think, my lord, that after fulfilling your request, I will have no more favors to do for you." And with that, he agrees to carry Todong's message. Todong looks at the monk for some time and then nods.

To Todong's relief, the abbot does agree to his proposal, and so they issue a proclamation stating that the impending dissolution of King Gesar's bodily form is to be moved two days later. But also they state that since Gesar's death is encouraging various maras and demons to bring doubt into the hearts of the people of Ling, and in order to protect the people, exorcisms and protector offerings will be performed outside the tent where Gesar sits in state.

This is done, and soon the sounds of horns and crashing cymbals resound louder than ever in the valley of Ling. The ceremonies themselves are very colorful, and the throngs of visitors feel their misgivings ebb away. After two more days, the ever-expanding encampment seems once again like a great fair.

*

Encountering the Shambhala Rulers

In the midnight darkness, Gesar still can hear men still drinking and muttering, but even to save himself, he cannot move. The world around him is ever more pathetic, sordid and remote. Imprisoned in his body, inert, utterly alone, he feels abandoned even by his great steed Kyang Ko Kar Kar. He has no desire to live and slowly feels himself leave his body once again. His spirit seems to detach itself and drifts upward. Then he is being carried upward on the night wind as if riding his faithful horse, Kyang Ko Kar Kar. Beneath him, Ling unfolds beneath him like a vast carpet of velvet valleys, silver mountain peaks, and rivers that flow like rivulets of mercury. Eddies of cold air burn his skin; sometimes it is painful, but other times it is a delight to feel so alive.

Suddenly Shambhala's high mountain range, glowing in starlight, loom up before him like a crystal wall. Twisting violently, he swerves upwards, and momentarily everything goes black. Then he blinks to flick a snowflake from his eye, and it is dawn.

Gesar finds himself near the center of a dazzling square courtyard larger than a parade ground. Its walls are covered with sheets of amethyst that glow like the sky at first light. A wide verandah of gold and jade on all four sides shines like hillsides touched by the rising sun. Its floors are black cedar and its columns vermilion with golden capitols. Four great doors, in the cardinal directions are also gold. Their cornices are fashioned from white jade and embossed with Tigers, Lions Garudas, and Dragons. The roof above is made of crystal tiles.

At the far end of the courtyard stands a high throne, carved from a single block of clear rock crystal and covered with a tiger skin. The scent of juniper incense fills the air, and the light is bright and even. It seems to Gesar that it is neither night nor day, but some bright time beyond either.

Gesar smiles as he realizes he is in the Amethyst Pavilion, the very center of the Kalapa Court. A sudden clack of cedar blocks stops his thoughts. Pungent juniper smoke fills the air, and high-pitched reeds play an hypnotic, undulating chord. The procession of the thirty-two Rulers of Shambhala begins, as one by one they enter slowly through the Eastern gate.

Gesar drops to his knees and puts his head to the glittering ground. In a slow regular rhythm an old man with a deep rumbling voice chants this salutation to the Rigdens. In great splendor, each dressed in robes of brocade, wearing golden crowns, and faintly jingling golden bracelets, they move along the black cedar floor.

As the radiant Lords of Kalapa emerge
From the golden Eastern gate of the Amethyst Pavilion,
The sun of time blazes:
This is the Vajra Time of nowness.

Time unfolds as twining vowels and consonants
Binding the senses and the elements.
Thus the Rigden Fathers join heaven and earth,
Show the true path of karma, cause and effect.
The virtues of the human realm
Resound like a great drum with their footfall.

The thirty-two Lords of Kalapa
Move slowly across the cedar floor.
Each in his time is sole ruler:
His unchanging inner radiance blazes
Through the shimmering clouds of time and space.
Each resolves one into the other,
As rays of golden light resolve into a single sun.

KI

As the procession of the thirty-two Lords of Shambhala courses clockwise past him
and around the porticos of the four directions of the Amethyst Pavilion, the Imperial
Ladies of Shambhala emerge from the Eastern gate wearing silver crowns and long
gowns of pale silk. Their jewels tinkle like little bells, and a faint perfume of lotus
flowers fills the air as they glide in and out of the line of sovereigns. A young woman's
high clear voice sings this:

As the radiant Queens of Kalapa emerge
From the golden Eastern gate of the Amethyst Pavilion,
The red sky flower of Time unfolds:
This is the Vajra Time of unceasing mahasukha.

Time spins with the vowels and consonants
Binding the senses and the elements.
Thus the Mother lineage offers
The true path of the senses,

And the endless union of heaven, earth and humankind.
The mercy of the human realm
Whispers with their footfall.

Each offers a world.
Each resolves one into the other,
As rays of silver light resolve into a single moon.

SO

Gesar feels as if he is suspended in the center of unimaginable radiant truth. Each of the Shambhala lords, moving slowly around the pavilion's verandah, is as dazzling as a sun coursing through the sky. The Imperial Ladies of Shambhala glow from within like the light of the moon. He is spellbound as if he is in the middle of the sky while sun and moon move in their orbits and cycles, from dawn to just after sunset, from winter through the four seasons, displaying at each moment a different kind of light around him.

*

The Dharma King Suchandra

Gesar is so dazzled that he loses all track of time. He does not realize that all but one of the rulers have completed the procession and withdrawn. As high reeds and silver cymbals play a melody that sounds like a wind high above the clouds, this ruler, the first sovereign of Shambhala ascends the crystal throne.

This is the first among the Dharma Kings of Shambhala whose name, resounding like thunder across an empty plain, is Suchandra, Auspicious Moon, the Lord of Secrets, the first son of King Suryaprabha and Queen Vijaya.

He is in the fullness of young manhood and his face is the color and texture of white jade. His expression is serene and completely unmoving, and the gaze of his eyes, dark and glittering like black volcanic glass, is acute and fathomless. His hair and mustache are black and smooth. He wears the Gold Crown of Reality Beyond the Limit of Knowledge; it is surmounted by a white diamond, free of any flaw.

As the lord of intuition and intellectual understanding, he wears gold earrings shaped like sea-dragons. His robe is turquoise adorned with golden tigers. His sash is pale yellow like an early winter moon. In his right hand he holds a white lotus on which stands a crystal Vajra. In his left, he holds silver bell. He sits on the glowing crystal throne beneath the rainbow-colored parasol of complete fearlessness that is vast as the sky.

Gazing at him, Gesar is overwhelmed as if he has emerged in the night from a narrow mountain pass and finds himself suddenly on an immense plain bathed in full moonlight.

This is the Great Dharma King who, at the great Stupa of Dyanataka, with the sure meekness of a tiger, prostrated his body to the Enlightened One, Sage of the Sakyas, Gautama Buddha, the conqueror of the three worlds and light of the present age.

This Dharma Raja then requested the teachings on the path of enlightenment for one who remains a King on earth, who remains in the embrace of the senses and lives a worldly life. He requested the teachings that show outer life as an inner path. He requested the teachings that open the gate of the seventh consciousness, and unfold the spontaneous wisdom of the ayatanas. He requested that the World Honored One show the world of basic goodness: brilliant, clear and fertile in the light of the Great Eastern Sun. In this way, he requested the Tathagatha to show how the Kingdom of Shambhala could simultaneously be a human realm and a pure realm.

When he made this request, the interior of the Stupa of Dyanataka became transformed into an immeasurable kapala as the inconceivable sphere of the Dharmadhatu. There, in the infinite expanse without beginning or end, The Completely Awakened One arose in the form Vajrasattva and opened the mandala of Kalachakra, the Primordial Buddha, The Lord of Time.

In the great dance of Vajra compassion, the Buddha opened the immeasurable palace: he displayed the twelve blissful aspects of the Lord of the Vajradhatu Proclamation and the sixteen mandalas of stars above. All this was unseen, unheard and unknown since the eon of Buddha Dipankara.

Thus, from the infinite treasury of the Buddha's body, speech and mind, this great jewel of teaching was given into the Dharma Rajah Suchandra's hand, and from him it flowed out into the world like a river of light. His outer and inner nature became one display given to all who encountered him.

As Gesar stares at this great Shambhala king, it seems that Suchandra's body slowly becomes translucent and within it, first faintly and then quite clearly, his inner secret form can be seen.

The unchanging secret form of the Great Dharma King Suchandra emanates from the Vajrapani, Lord of Action. He is ever youthful, and his unclothed body is white as a conch. His face is inviting and completely peaceful. Because he has attained the summit of dharma, he wears a top-knot surmounted by the three jewels, blazing with their own radiance.

He wears the garland crown of the five senses displayed as flowers and a necklace of the five elements displayed as five kinds of gemstones. He wears a red and gold brocade shawl as radiant as the splendor of love. His golden bracelets are the four aims of life. He wears the Jewel Treasure of the Ocean on a gold chain at his heart. In his right hand, he holds the Wish Fulfilling Tree, and in his left a red lotus on which stood the golden eight-spoked wheel of unobstructed truth surmounted by the three jewels.

On his right, his consort, gold as the dawn sun, named Golden Ground of Illusory Display, holds the gold vase of eternal life surmounted by the flaming three jewels. All the offerings of the phenomenal world are spread out before them. In the peace of his radiance, there is no room for doubt or discursiveness.

Suchandra, the Great King of Shambhala sits without moving, and Gesar is unable even to blink. He cannot tell if this Dharma King is outside himself, something deep within him, or beyond such a distinction.

The Dharma King's consort suddenly shakes her head and a luxurious cascade of dark hair flows across her naked shoulder. Gesar's mind flickers. A strong scent of some unknown musky perfume wafts over him. Gesar looks over at her, and sees an expression of slight impatience on her delicate face. Suddenly anxious, he looks up at the sovereign, and as he does so a flash of light reflecting from the diamond on the great lord's crown blinds him, and floods his entire being.

Gesar quivers as a cold breeze runs across his chest. With a sharp pang of anguish, he realizes he is still in Ling. The night has become cold, and the moon, high in the dark sky, has begun to set. Galaxies of stars thick as a blizzard fill the sky. His body and the world around him feel completely linked. At that moment, his whole existence is nothing but a prayer.

The Buddha, the Completely Awakened One
Has displayed his body as the universe
And shown the nature of the world,
As being the nature of his body,
As being awake.

Seeing, hearing, smelling, taste, touch and consciousness
Blaze out and burn like a torch.
Their light fills all of space.
The Four Great Elements dance in the light of the senses
And shape the world.

This is the direct experience of enlightenment as body,
The inseparable ground of duality and non-duality.

The senses flow outward,
Endlessly outward in a tide of rainbow light.
There is nowhere to return.
This is the awakened state at the level of body.

The accumulations of the skandhas,
The constant effort to own experience,
And the futile struggle for identity and self
Are constantly dispersed.
This is called the bardo of life,
Which contains the bardos of dream and of meditation.

The outward race of the senses creates dreams
Which no one can sustain,
And creates life which no one can sustain.
Meditations which distinguish
Between Shamatha and Vipassana,
Between meditation and non-meditation
Cannot be sustained.

The centerless expansion of the ayatanas is the bardo of life,
The direct experience of the awakened state as body.
There is no one and nowhere to return to.

Here within in the bonfire of the senses
The elements shine.
From the glow of blue light spreading,
The element of space expands.
From the glow of white light extending,
The element of water spontaneously cools and flows.
From the glow of yellow light pervading,
The element of earth spontaneously enriches and solidifies.
From the glow of red light engaging,
The element of fire spontaneously warms and rises.
From the dark glow of green light consuming,
The element of wind swirls and roars.

Perception does not create a center
And the mandala of the elements
Unsought and unoriginated,
Arising only in nowness itself,
Moves and fills the whole of space.

The time of the body is impermanence.
This is the experience of the Bardo of Life,

The direct experience of the awakened state as embodiment.
Living this way, one is like a tiger
Who leaps through the air and does not look back.

Gesar feels light and joyful, and, smiling, he falls asleep.

*

On a foggy morning four days before Gesar's funeral, Lord Todong sits in his tent taking his breakfast of yogurt, bread and tea and preparing for his daily visit to the settlement around Gesar's tent.

He is pleased at the progress building the tall white crematory stupa in which Gesar's body will be burned, but he is not entirely satisfied with the nearby camp. Despite his soldiers' best efforts, a certain rowdy atmosphere seems to be growing. Certainly, many people spend their days meditating and praying, but many others are becoming restless and seek diversion in gambling, wrestling, archery contests, eating and drinking. At Todong's request, the Abbot has posted schedules for practice and proclaimed rules of conduct, but these appear to have little effect. Todong is afraid that a riot of dissolute behavior will bode ill for his prospects as future king of Ling. And even though Gesar's loyalists seem broken for now, Todong knows they are capable of stirring up trouble at the slightest opportunity. Truly, Todong sighs, the trials of a ruler are endless.

As he is musing disconsolately about this state of affairs, a small caravan appears out of the mist and stops before his tent. Two gaudy carts with faded gold wheels, each painted all the colors of the rainbow and pulled by a piebald yak, clatter up, then groan to a halt. A dozen or so men and women, all outlandishly dressed in pointed hats and bright ragged robes dismount from their goats and donkeys and shake themselves to relieve the rigors of a long journey.

A tall, broad shouldered man, dusty and mud-spattered, follows them. His face as dark red, his eyes pale blue and bloodshot, and his hair, though dirty, is reddish gold. He wears a round hat with a broad circular brim made of maroon leather, and his cape is a faded crimson. Beneath his cape he wears black armor dotted with rust. A broadsword with a gilded grip hangs from his waist, and a mothy leopard skin quiver and black bow are strapped to his saddle. He rides on a large white nag with twisted ears.

Todong's wife Kurzar Sartog and Methok Lhadze hear the racket and come out to join their lord. What they see amazes them. As the slatternly men and women of this rag-tag entourage sprawl on the ground without the slightest display of respect, the tall man dismounts and approaches Todong. His slightly mocking smile reveals long and very white teeth, which are somehow even more disconcerting than his bold manner.

"Hail great Todong, Prince of ten thousand warriors and King of Ling," and with this he makes a flamboyantly low bow. Todong is both irritated by the effrontery of the stranger and flattered by his words. He waves his hand vaguely for the man to continue.

"I and my friends have traveled across the entire earth, but hearing of King Gesar's death we have raced day and night to reach here now. We once met the Great King and wish to honor him. Wherever we have traveled, your fame, Sire, and your reputation for valor and wisdom are renowned. Thus we also wish the honor of serving you in this great time of loss."

"And how precisely could the likes of you, whatever you are, be of any service to me?"

"Ah, sire, I know we look like an unreliable and foolish lot, but that is the fate of those who make their livelihood as we do."

"And that is?"

"Oh great King, we are performers. Everywhere from the great cities of China to the hamlets of India, from the palaces of emperors, the yurts of the khans of the steppes, and the gold pavilions of rajas, to the houses of merchants, and fairgrounds and parks teeming with the poor we present the great sagas of the Pandava, of Rama, and of King Gesar."

"And so..."

"Sire, as we passed through the camp of those who have come to Gesar's funeral, we could not help but notice a certain restlessness, a certain amount of disrespectful sport. Though we came here with no intention of plying our trade, it seemed to us that perhaps, if under your auspices, we presented an entertainment more in keeping with this sorrowful occasion, a tale from King Gesar's heroic and eventful life, the crowd would be moved to awe and pity. A more harmonious atmosphere might prevail."

Despite his misgivings at the troupe's raffish appearance, this proposal makes some sense to Todong, and he is about to accede, when his wife and Methok Lhadze pulls him aside.

"This is a trick," hisses Kurzar Sartog, "These people are professional frauds. Nothing good will come of sponsoring them."

"This is Gesar's doing, I'm sure of it." Methok Lhadze wails.

"She's right, " Todong's wife nods, agreeing with her daughter-in-law for once. And turning to Todong, she continues; "Always you fall for these gimmicks. Gesar has laid these traps for you many times, and you always fall for them."

"He is dead, and I am alive," snarls Todong. "If I'm such a fool, explain that."

But then the stranger interrupts smoothly:

"Sire, it is not our wish to create discord in your household or anywhere else. Seeing the trouble we have already made, we will pay our respects to your former monarch and make our way to the Emperor of China who sent for us some time ago."

"I make the decisions here," roars Todong, glaring at the women and at the performers. "You are not leaving yet. I will have a spot cleared for you, and you will set up whatever kind of stage you need. You will begin your performance tomorrow evening. And I will be there for every bit of it, so don't try anything second rate."

And with that, the tall man smiles, bows, and departs with his caravan into the fog.

*

The Great Dharma King, the First Rigden Manjusri Yasas

Lying half asleep, half awake, Gesar overhears the stranger and smiles. He dozes off, and, as if he were dissolving into a warm dark river, he feels himself carried off on its relentless current. When he opens his eyes, he is once again in the Kalapa Court.

Gesar is wearing his gold robe, crown and his armor of bronze. He sits on a gilded campstool on a clearing covered with moonstones amid a garden filled with peach trees. Ripe peaches glisten with dew, and beneath them deep banks of fragrant white peonies float on waves of dark glossy leaves. Yellow finches flitter in the branches, and the air is warm, humid, clean and sweet. Before him golden carp swim lazily in a shallow pool. Beyond the pool in a larger clearing, stands a high golden throne surmounted by dragons carved from green jade. Behind the throne, an immense tree spreads its emerald branches adorned with flowers of many-colored jewels.

A flute far off plays a haunting melody. Suddenly from a path beside the throne appears, alone and without retinue, the First of the Imperial Rigdens, Manjusri Yasas, Renowned Friend of Manjusri.

During this great Dharma Rajah's reign in Shambhala, many of his subjects in each of the four castes followed teachings other than the Buddha's. Their disputes grew and provoked uncertainty throughout the kingdom. The great lord then proclaimed his intention to unite all secular and spiritual paths in the single and unchanging ground of basic goodness, and thus to unite all beings in one single Vajra caste.

But those who insisted on holding the ways of their forebears left to go to their ancient homeland in the South. The Lord of Great Renown saw that this too would bring disrepute both to the teachings and the kingdom of Shambhala. So he flew through the cold winter air, and appeared before them on the highway where they walked. He appeared not as a vision, but as himself, seated on his throne in his garden in the palace of Kalapa.

Because he is the Lord of Speech, this great Rigden dances freely in space. His mind is unobstructed by the distinction between form and formlessness, attainment and obstacle. As the Lord of Speech, he is master of the vowels and consonants, the red and white elements, and the outer experiences of space as near and far. His compassion manifests completely and concretely without any concessions to mere appearance. Thus, likewise, the Kingdom of Shambhala can manifest completely anywhere in space and time.

Manjusri Yasas then transported those who were leaving back to Kalapa, and they awoke as from a dream in the great pleasure garden of Malaya. There, the Great Earth Protector Sovereign showed the sign of EVAM, the heart of the Primordial Buddha, the indivisibility of space and phenomena revealed in the union of the vowels and consonants.

Hearing the Rigden's words and seeing his display, those who had been inclined to follow the way of the Vedas were freed from clinging to their own history, and caste. They saw the face of reality, free from veils or obscurity. They saw the Rigden's presence as the spontaneous mandala of the inseparable Body, Speech and Mind of the Primordial Awakened State. They had no desire for any other path.

Thus this great lord became the first in the line of Rigden Kings, the first in the line of the twenty-five who Hold the Caste, the first in a line that shines like the sun through all the shifting clouds of time. Thus Rigden Manjusri-Yasas established the pure expanse of nowness inseparable from the totality of all phenomena as the golden ground of the human realm.

As Gesar sits unmoving and unwavering, the Great Dharma Lord slowly takes his seat upon his throne.

The Dharma Lord Manjusri-Yasas sits before the wish-fulfilling tree on a gold throne that blazes like the noonday sun. His skin is the color of sunrise, and his eyes are blue and piercing. His expression is fresh and completely alert. His black mustache and hair are elegantly arranged. He wears the gold brocade turban and gold crown of a dharma king, surmounted by a blue diamond bright as the sky just before dawn. He wears an outer turquoise robe embroidered with golden lions. His under robe is made from spun gold. His sash is red like the first light on a mountain peak, and he wears the gold necklaces, earrings, and bracelets of an earth-protector. In his right hand, he holds the stem of a lotus on which rests the flaming vajra sword that, instantaneously and without moving, cuts through the darkness of ignorance. Because the treasury of true wisdom is never lost, in his left hand, he holds aloft a text.

Encountering him, Gear is suddenly filled with energy, as if he had never known uncertainty or self-doubt. And as he gazes at the great Earth Protector, Gesar sees, blazing from within, the changeless form of Manjusri Yasas' inner nature.

His body is red, the color of a glowing ember. His compassionate gaze completely encompasses all the form and the formless realms. In his soft smile there is not the slightest hint of separation from anything.

He wears the jeweled crown of the five tathagathas, and, because absolute and relative truth are indestructibly united, a gold five-pointed vajra is braided in his topknot. His body is naked to the waist and adorned with the necklaces, bracelets and earrings, showing his complete power over the senses. He wears red pants and a sky blue skirt embroidered with stars. In his right hand, he holds the stem of a lotus on which rested a blazing vajra sword. In his left hand he holds a text containing the essence of all that can be known. Because all the lineages of kama and terma are inseparable from his being, he holds his two hands crossed at his heart.

He sits amid clouds of rainbow lights that emanate from his pores and pervade the whole of space with the radiance of sutra and tantra. He is seated on a cinnabar throne supported by four blue and four white lions. His consort on his left named Drum of Truth is the dark green of complete accomplishment. She holds a lotus of ever expanding compassion in her left hand, while with her right she makes the mudra that brings fearlessness to all.

Lost in amazement, Gesar suddenly realizes that the Rigden is looking at him. The gaze of those sapphire-bright eyes is so curious, so neutral, that Gesar quickly looks away. But when he glances furtively at the Great Ruler, he is dazzled by a sphere of red light, burning like a setting sun, blazing out from the Rigden's throat. A stream of sparks burst through the air and enter Gesar's throat. He feels he is choking. He coughs and desperately tries to catch his breath. Suddenly he wakes back in Ling.

Far off in the night a breeze begins to rise. Without moving, Gesar looks around. Torches are guttering. Sechan Dugmo is deep asleep. Slowly all his feelings of love, regret, rage, joy, sorrow, exultation coalesce as a ceaseless flow. Overwhelmed by emotion, this song fills his heart:

The Buddha, the Completely Awakened One,
Has enunciated the truth as the vowels and consonants,
Articulating all phenomena,
Their origin, their relationships and their end.
The path of enlightenment unfolds without limit or end
As non-duality expresses itself directly in duality.

Carried on the living breath of the awakened state,
The sheer intensity of unceasing communication
In all the experiences of being born, living, dying and giving birth
Is the speech of the Awakened One.

All the identities of self and other
And all the relationships between
Expand and contract as the experience of time.
This is the play of the vowels and consonants.

As the vowels and consonants
Join, swirl and echo through the whole of space,
The biased designations of truth and delusion, existence and non-existence,

Memory, history, meaning, and implications,
Are shaped, stabilized, changed, destroyed.
This is the direct expression of enlightenment as speech,
The continuous experience of the bardos of dying and luminosity.

In any moment when one does not actively perpetuate a view,
Gaps spontaneously open,
The net of habitual ideas, assumptions and beliefs wavers,
And one has nothing to hold to.

As mental constructs dissolve back into the vowels and consonants,
A great roaring a tornado paralyzes the mind.
One is drawn on and can neither manipulate nor escape.
The three kinds of discursive thought cease.

As sound and silence cannot finally be distinguished,
An all-consuming brilliance
Moves like sheet lightening and fills the whole of space.
This is the totality of primordial utterance.

Now like a lion sinking claws and fangs
Into the back of a wild horse,
Shout the warrior cry of KI and SO.
Without holding back,
Without even clinging to consciousness,
Seize the wind of time.

The time of speech is continuity.
In this way,
By means of the Bardo of dying and of luminosity,
Accept the direct empowerment
Of the uncontrived Speech of the Awakened One.

*

Over the following afternoon, evening, night and day, the troupe of performers sets to work in a large clearing beside the tent where Gesar's body sits. Their exotic dress and easy ways, not to mention the strange structure they are in the process of erecting attracts a small herd of bored of children who soon run errands for them. Later older children come along, and then their parents. Soon everyone in the camp comes by to see what these genial strangers are up to, and speculates about what kind of event they will present.

On the evening of the performance, the air is cool. Warm breezes carry the scent of dry leaves and hay. A crescent moon and galaxies of stars float in the lavender sky. From all directions, crowds buzzing with anticipation stream towards the impromptu theater. When they arrive, they find that the circumference of the clearing is marked with a great circle of torches, and the space just outside is ringed with food stalls. Quickly then, they buy food and find places on the ground to sit.

The stage, a large square of polished golden pine four feet off the ground is oddly imposing. Brightly colored banners depicting the kings of the four directions hang on either side. Behind, a high white screen conceals the rear of the stage.

When the crowd is settled and all the enclosure filled, Todong makes his entrance. He is dressed in a robe of gold brocade adorned with red tigers, and he takes his seat on an ebony throne set up for him directly in front of the stage. His son in a smoke colored silk robe, his wife in green satin, and his daughter-in-law in pink brocade adorned with lotus blossoms sit beside him on either side.

In the darkness, Sechan Dugmo, accompanied by the old prime minister, Tseshang Denma, Odkar Gyaltsen, Gesar's heir, and the few other loyal ministers enter quietly and sit on a small platform to the side of the clearing. Only those nearby notice them.

After the crowd has once again become still, a stagehand lights rows of small candles down each side and across the front of the stage. Then the tall stranger, now dressed in a simple black silk robe, steps out onto the stage and walks slowly down to the front left. His expression is impassive and, as he stares out into the audience, it seems he gazes at each woman, man, and child. Then two men and two women, also dressed in black, carrying percussion, stringed and wind instruments, follow him. They stand as he places dried juniper on a pot filled with embers at the center stage, and the incense of the tree of life fills the air. The performers sit down in a row along one side of the stage and arrange their instruments. The stranger, as troupe leader, sits nearest the audience.

An oil light is lit behind the screen and flickers at its center. Slowly the light grows in intensity, losing its own outline and spreading until the screen is suffused with an even golden glow. The troupe leader then turns to the audience and addresses them in a simple unaffected voice:

"Here in this world, obscured by ignorance and hatred, greed, lust, and ambition, the landscape of the four great elements and the deeds of the great pure heroes are seen only as shadows. Their words here are heard only as the echo of the truth."

As he speaks, the valley of Ling and the river through it, appear in silhouette, and when he says the word 'heroes', Gesar's silhouette appears suddenly and clearly on a high peak above the valley.

The audience breaks out in delighted laughter and applauds at this wonder. Todong turns to his wife. "See, see," he whispers, "It's going to be all right." Then the stranger turns his side to the audience, the instrumentalists begin to play, and in a strong melodious voice, he chants.

At a time when the future seems most perilous:
When there is no clear refuge,
When the truth has degenerated,
Teachers are self-seeking, friends and loved ones fickle,
Then, on the occasion of sickness, death, or battle,
This invocation to Gesar, Norbu Dradul is sung.
Offering billows of juniper smoke,
We sing this with the music of cymbals and drums.

And with this, the stranger sings an invocation to Gesar, King of Ling. He then recounts the story of King Gesar's journey to save his mother Dzeden be traversing the realms of life and death.

While he narrates, his voice alters to convey each character and place, while on the screen behind him the images of Gesar, Kyang Ko Kar Kar, Sechan Dugmo and all the rest appear in silhouette, gesturing, moving, dancing, all bringing the words to life.

As the shadow puppets move closer to the screen, their outlines become sharply detailed; even the colors of their faces and clothes tint the shadows. When they are tilted to one side or another or up or down, their expressions seem to change. And when the shadow puppets are moved back farther from the screen, they seem to dissolve in the light. So as word and image merge, the audience is transported into the intense shadow world before them. The voices and songs, floating through the cold night air, seem truly to be the inner movements of their hearts. In the deepening night, the shadow images unfold in the darkness and assume spectral three-dimensional shapes.

When Sechan Dugmo hears Manene's song, she weeps, for finally she begins to see why her husband has had to leave her behind. At Dzeden's lament, even Todong and his family drop their haughty expressions and are moved to tears. Likewise, Gesar's sorrow moves everyone, as if he were standing stricken before them. At such moments, Odkar Gyaltsen has the strange sensation that rather than being entranced, he is waking up.

Then, as Gesar moves from earth to water to fire to wind, darkness seems to assume those forms, engulfing every being in the crowd, oppressing them, flowing around them, burning and drawing them on and stripping them to the marrow. They feel as if they are falling through the world.

But after they see Kyang Ko Kar Kar bring the great lord's body to Ling, while Gesar journeys into the worlds of life and death, the audience realizes with shock, that they are seeing what has happened in their own lives at the same time. They are seeing the great voyage of King of Ling has undertaken while all thought him dead. This is the truth of what has happened in the last half year, and they feel ashamed.

Sechan Dugmo grips the prime minister's hand fiercely, and Gesar's old ministers grin. Todong's wife glares at her husband, but he fidgets with his handkerchief and affects not to notice.

The growling sound of cymbals and the wail of horns shakes the watchers out of their reflections and private thoughts. And as a deep voiced chorus chants the invocation to Vetali, and again a stagehand placed another set of offerings across the front of the stage, many feel as if they too are looking at the horizon of life and death. And yet there is nothing to be seen. The screen at the back of the stage is almost black and the stage as well, but something in the darkness itself seems alive and terrifying. Silence seems to swallow the night. Then the stranger begins to chant alone.

Gesar, King of Ling was never moved from wakefulness
By birth and death.
In endless journeys and battles
To liberate all human kind
He had never passed through the shadows
Of the bardos and realms.

But now Gesar's love for the one who gave him birth,
The Naga Princess Dzeden
Draws him onto that treacherous path.
So he enters into the kingdom of Yama, the Lord of Death.

Then, like a great breaking wave of visions and dreams, the story of Gesar's encounter with the Lord of Death and his passage through the six realms engulfs all the audience. As the sounds and images envelop them, they do not know whether they are in the time of the story or in their own time, or if the experience of Gesar and Kyang Ko Kar Kar are the experience of another or their own. They do not know whether the episodes in Ling that they have witnessed themselves or heard of from friends are the true ones or a pale comedy played out while a deeper drama took place.

At times, as the endless playing of cymbals, shrieking reeds, snare drums, flutes, horns, tam tams, bass drums and strings fill their ears, and the ceaseless images of the realms fly before their eyes, they only want it to stop. But all feel the gateway to their own Hell, and within their own craving a hidden Preta Realm; in their fear-born dreams, they sense the stirrings of Animal instincts, and the great display of the Humans rouse their own pride. The striving of the Asuras are a mirror of their own ambition, and the varying bliss of Gods appears as their own deepest aim.

At the conclusion of Gesar's journey through the realms, the narrator turns to the audience, and again it seems to each that he is looking only at her or him as he says:

"Know that these realms are simultaneous and each fills the whole of space. Because of your karma and the state of your perceptions you cannot see them all. But all the realms exist here right now. Some animals, of course, you see, but countless others are too small for your sight. Likewise beings of the Hell and Hungry Ghost realms press close to you in every instant of the day and night. Asuras and Gods dazzle your imagination and touch you with their exaltation. When the gods and goddesses touch you with their desires, your mind is filled with bliss. In a breeze, a sudden rage, a scent, longing, the chill of fear, an unaccountable moment of happiness, a pocket of warm air beside a riverbank, a feeling of horror, a shadow seen from the corner of your eye, you may know this."

But whatever momentary tremor this statement causes is dispelled as the audience watch Gesar and his mother together with the Miracle Horse Kyang Ko Kar Kar descend into the Naga realm, returning to the palace which was Dzeden's childhood home. There accompanied by the soft mournful sounds of flutes and the slow beating of drums, Dzeden sings her last song. And so, at last when the time came for Dzeden to die, weep and fall into exhausted sorrow.

Again, as the action returns to Ling, the environment seems cruder and more simple-minded. The audience feels increasingly uneasy. But this mood shifts at the solemn cadences of hand drums and bells accompanying Gesar's last liturgy for his mother. At the end of this section, the light behind the screen becomes ever brighter until the whole space seems an ocean of bright gold. Into this light steps a young girl, dressed in pink brocades with silver trim. She bows quickly to the audience, smiles shyly, and makes her speech.

Now that Gesar's toils have been revealed,
It's to your present needs we shall appeal.
We, the actors need some rest
And in our absence we think it best
For you to get some food and drink.
We will resume, quick as a wink.
But for a moment, free from strife,
Enjoy the pleasures of this human life.

And with that, she curtsies. The lights behind the stage go out, and the musicians and singers sweep off the stage. Everyone in the audience is slightly stunned, and blinks as if they all have just waked up. Many sit unmoving and lost in thought, many are simply tired for it is very late, and many others make their way to the food stalls and the wine sellers.

Methok Lhadze is upset, and she turns to look through the crowd to see if people are thinking badly of her. Most are now chatting with their neighbors or sitting quietly or eating fried bread and drinking rice wine or tea. But off to the side in shadow, she catches Sechan Dugmo's eye. Gesar's wife stares at her with unwavering coldness until the flighty princess is forced to look away.

"We must leave now," she whispers urgently and pulls at Todong's sleeve. But Todong is busy eating from a plate of roast meat, and waves her off. She tries to catch her husband's attention, but he is laughing with the Prince of Hor at the latter's unflattering appearance in the play. Methok Lhadze then tries to appeal to her mother in law, but her seat is empty.

Gesar's general, Chopa Tongden observes all this, and nudges Tsashang Denma. "Soon the fur will fly," he whispers. But a gong sounds announcing the resumption of the performance, and the old general is pleased to note that people are no longer so anxious to be seated near Todong and his entourage. In fact there is a quite a lot of empty space around them now.

*

The Great Dharma King Pundarika

The night is sparkling now and peaceful. The velvet depth of darkness muffle the voices of the actors, but Gesar can feel, if only faintly, the excitement of the audience. He smiles and closes his eyes, but when he tries to sleep, he feels restless. He is powerless to resist the stream of hallucinations that now carry him from one world to another. Thus he finds that once again he is in Kalapa on the roof of the Kalapa Court itself.

The roof of the Court is composed of many small crystal panels. They absorb light by day and emit light by night, and through night and day they sparkle like a calm sea. It is as hot as high summer, but a light breeze blows carrying the scent of peonies and the tinkling sound of the many small bells that hang in the palace eaves. Iridescent butterflies, some the color of peacock's wings, others like opals flutter in the air. Somewhere someone is playing the ghanta and damaru.

Gesar is seated on a small throne of cinnabar on a large platform covered in white raw silk. Beside him on a cinnabar table is a tray of meat dumplings, hot sauce, a bowl of yogurt, a jade teapot and cup, a crystal goblet, and a crystal carafe of rice wine.

Facing him, against a background of towering white clouds and seated on the gold eight-lion throne of Shambhala is the second Imperial Rigden, Pundarika, the White Lotus Cherished by Avalokiteshvara. It was he whose impetuous compassion broke the barrier between pure and impure realms. This then is the Rigden who, like a great Garuda soaring through space, extends the Shambhala teachings beyond the borders of Shambhala itself and spreads them throughout the human realm.

In the clear pale light of early dawn, Gesar is surprised that the Earth Protector

Sovereign is so very young and that he is simply having breakfast. The Great King smiles mischievously and gestures to his guest to eat. Gesar looks at the carafe, then back at the Sovereign who nods. He is disconcerted by the sovereign's informality and, as he eats the food beside him, he is careful not to dine more quickly or more slowly than the Rigden.

The Rigden Pundarika sits on the gold eight-lion throne of Shambhala. He is very youthful and his skin is white and clear as a mother of pearl. His eyes are like obsidian, and he looks on the world around him with a tender smile. He wears the gold crown of a dharma king at the apex of which is set a white opal that glows in the patterns and colors of all the realms.

His robe is the pale orange of first light embroidered with golden garudas. His sash is the dark blue of cloudless winter sky. He wears the gold necklaces, earrings, and bracelets of an earth-protector.

When the Rigden sits back for a moment and crosses his hands at his heart, all the atoms of his being radiate warmth and unconditional love. And in that moment, it seems that in his hands he holds the green stem of a white lotus which blossoms like a cloud in the morning sky. And, as Gesar watches, the inner form of the Imperial Rigden glows like a sun. All the outer world becomes pale and insubstantial.

In his unchanging inner form, the Rigden Pundarika is pale as moonlight and his expression gentle and at ease. In the topknot of his black hair is the Buddha himself. As the master of all meditations of form, he wears a gold meditation belt on his right shoulder. As the master of meditations not reliant on form, he wears the skin of a blue antelope over his left shoulder. In his right hand, he holds a mala made of pearls and in his left a stem from which a pink lotus in full bloom unfolded.

Naked to the waist, he wears a red skirt embroidered with swirling clouds and orange pants embroidered with countless golden suns. He sits on a circular golden throne, and his feet rest on moon disks that float on a crimson lotus. On his left, his golden consort, named Seal of Union, holds her hands in angeli.

Because every movement of his mind is selfless love, because every thought that rises spontaneously in his mind is the innate freedom of every sentient being, he is the golden ocean of unconditional fearlessness. He is the Mahasukhakhaya, the form of bliss of all the Buddhas. He is the Great Eastern Sun.

Suddenly, the Rigden Pundarika, seeing the needs of beings and the shape of time, in a high piercing voice like the cry of a hawk, cries out "KIIIIIIIIII", and the sound shakes and echoes in the whole of the sky. Then without taking a breath, his voice drops and, resounding like an avalanche in a narrow ravine, he shakes all the earth: "SO SO SO SO SO SO SO SO SO." Heaven and Earth reverberate together like a great golden bell.

Abruptly the young Rigden becomes silent and sips some tea. He peers over his cup at Gesar and smiles shyly. Gesar realizes that he has neglected to taste his own tea, and without looking, picks up his cup and swallows. With a violent shock, he realizes that he has drunk the bowl of hot sauce. His face turns red as a furnace. His eyes bulge, and he begins to sweat in torrents. The Rigden bursts out laughing, and the tea in his mouth sprays all over Gesar, engulfing him in a wave of blue light that, at the same instant, sprang from the Rigden's heart.

Gesar's mind becomes a single blue dot inseparable from these words.

The Buddha has shown his mind
As the nature of reality itself.
All that is experienced as real,
Is the Buddha's mind.

Not reliant on the senses,
Not reliant on words and things,

The crystal razor edge of pure primordial awareness
Moves in the whole of space,
Moves in the senses,
Moves in concepts,
Moves in beings and realms.

Clear, vivid, empty, awake,
The razor of clear empty awareness
Shines as the radiance of the senses,
Cuts as the experience of the reality of phenomena,
Surges as the life force of beings and realms.

It cannot be named or described or encompassed in any way.
Empty clear awareness is inseparable from space itself.

The primordial stroke of the red Garuda's razor wing
Slices through measureless space and raises the winds of life.

Cut by the primordial stroke,
Mind is severed from individual preoccupation.
Body and mind are unified,
Illusory yet real,
In the instant form of illusion-emptiness.

This is immediate experience
Free from certainty or uncertainty.

The time of mind is duality itself.

Cut by the primordial stroke,
Mind is severed from individual preoccupations.
The sky flower of exterior phenomena
Unfolds spontaneously
As the mandala of wisdom deities and dralas.

This is the ceaseless experience of the world,
Shimmering, vivid, and ungraspable.

Here is the direct experience of the Bardo of Illusory Body
    and Dharmata,
The direct empowerment of the awakened state as mind,
The wisdom of prajna and compassion inseparable,
Living as the Garuda flies through measureless space.

Gesar opens his eyes. The stars are fading in the blue-black night, and the edge of dawn now glows a faint violet on the Eastern sky.

*

Even before all the spectators have returned to their seats, the light behind the screen is lit, and the play, now showing Todong's rule and the prosperity of Ling, has begun. However, the puppets have now been altered so that Todong looks more toad-like than human, his son more like a fox, his wife like a magpie, and his daughter-in-law like a cat. The people of Ling, so happy in their prosperity appear as a herd of fat sheep, and only those who remained loyal to Gesar retain their human form and heartfelt expression. No one knows whether to laugh or slink away, and all are relieved when the stage again darkens and the stranger, his steely voice, accompanied by chimes, drums, and deep gongs playing in undulant sound, begins to recite.

"The Unmatched and Unvanquished one, Gesar King of Ling manifests in this world as the Peerless Warrior. But truly it is said:

Through a thousand worlds, like a thousand suns
His great light blazes.

Without effort, he appears,
Summoned by the needs of myriad beings.
Spontaneously, he arises in myriad forms.

"Gesar appears in other realms as a single sun glitters all the myriad surfaces of the sea. You have seen him on this earth. You have watched his journeys through a thousand Hells, the Preta Realms, the Animal realms, and the innumerable realms of the Asuras and Gods. But even now Gesar takes his seat in the pure realm of Shambhala.

"This realm, this Kingdom of Shambhala is so close to you. You can almost feel it. But somehow it eludes you, even as you sense that your lives upon this earth should be just and dignified, completely passionate, completely inspired, completely awake. This is how you glimpse Shambhala, but fear and hope prevent you from making it reality."

Again the light blazes behind the screen and seems brighter than ever. The figures are even more clear and marvelous, the colors of their costumes more vivid, their gestures and movements more subtle and poignant. The ethereal sounds of reeds and drums seem to descend from the sky, and draw everyone in the audience into another realm.

What now they see where Gesar has ventured in his dreams, and it is as if it was their own dream. They see the Rigdens emerge one by one. They see the living faces of the Great Earth Protector Rigdens Suchandra, Manjusri-Yasas, and Pundarika. And then as Gesar dreams in his tent, the performers chant and dance the same things he now dreams. All the people of Ling enter the future time of the last Rigden, the all-conquering Raudracakrin.

*

The Final Rigden Raudracakrin

Gesar flies through darkness to the time of future prophecy. The world below him spins from the dark of night to the blazing light so rapidly it looks like a luminous blue pearl. As he reaches the time of the last Rigden, it is ferociously cold. Freezing gales tear at him and he is pelted by sharp snowflakes and shards of hale. In the distance, approaching like the dark roiling cloudbanks of a gathering storm, an immense celestial army of Gods and Asuras swirl in the sky. This maelstrom of purple, turquoise and black clouds pulses with flashes of lightening, the gleam of swords drawn, the roar of chariots and the whistle of arrows.

Slicing up through the heart of universal cowardice, the final Rigden bursts from the fastness of Kalapa like an iridescent dragon rising from a lake. The twenty-fifth Rigden of Shambhala, Raudracakrin, 'The Wrathful One Who Turns The Wheel', he who will end the time of strife and establish a new Golden Age takes his seat amid his army on a great turquoise charger with blue-black mane and tail. This great stallion's gold ornaments glitter, filling the sky with lightning bolts, and his stamping hooves shake the earth with thunder.

Rigden Raudracakrin is in the prime of manhood and his face and body are dark red. His obsidian eyes glare with imperious fury, and he snarls with rage. He wears the dazzling gold crown of a dharma king adorned with glowing emeralds and sapphires. His golden armor is blinding like the direct sight of the sun. Around his neck, on a white silk scarf, he wears a great crystal mirror in which all the phenomena of time and space arise and dissolve. Beneath his armor he wears a robe of green brocade with red sleeves lined in pale coral satin. His pants are red brocade adorned with golden dragons. His outer robe is red, gold and white brocade. A great lapis colored serpent twines round his neck falling to the level of his secret center. Green serpents trailing dark clouds encircle his wrists.

In his raised right hand, he brandishes the flaming spear that destroys the universe with kalpa-ending fire. The shaft of his spear is adorned with garudas' feathers and a swirling green and coral scarf. In his left hand he turns the eight pointed wheel of meteoric iron marked with eight great syllables, whose sound, as the wheel turns, destroys all false beliefs about reality and deafens the emotions of grasping and fixation.

At the sight of him, Gesar is terrified to the marrow and feels that suddenly he faces complete annihilation. He is unable to turn back or turn his gaze away from the world-ending Rigden, and as he stares in awe, the monarch seems, for an instant, transparent.

In his unchanging secret form, the Rigden Raudracakrin is the great protector, Manjusri, youthful and at ease. His red body is the color of an all-consuming sandalwood fire. Nothing in the form and formless worlds, in mind and beyond mind is separate from the light of his unwavering empty gaze. All distortions, upheavals, displays, realizations and freedom rest within his sovereign equipoise. All the winds of sky and earth are his soft voice, the secret speech of Samantabhadra pervading life and death.

As the absolute lord of all wisdom, he wears the gold and jeweled crown of the five Tathagathas. Because wisdom presence is inseparable from limitless compassion, his crown is surmounted by a ruby the size of Mount Meru.

Because the radiance of wisdom illuminates all phenomena, he wears necklaces, armbands, bracelets, and anklets of shining gold and glittering jewels. Entering into all the world's activities, he wears a billowing shawl of shimmering emerald green. His skirt is coral and decked with golden butterflies. His red silk pants are adorned with galaxies of suns and moons, and their blue lining is embellished with all the swirling clouds in space.

In his right hand, he holds at his heart in the mudra of teaching, the green stem of a fragrant pink lotus in full bloom on which stands the gold eight-spoked wheel of the law turning in a mass of flame. As the wheel turns, the claustrophobia of illusory reality is shown to be inseparable from all-pervasive, free, luminous bliss. In his left hand held at his heart in the mudra of ceaseless offering is the green stem of a vast pink lotus in full bloom. At its center stands the blazing sword of primordial awareness, cutting spontaneously through the pained half-light of conceptualization and revealing on the spot the infinite radiant empty space of liberation.

He is seated on a hexagonal cloud-backed throne of gold and cinnabar, supported by eight snow-lions, four the color of turquoise, four the color of conch. Above him sways a gold and vermilion parasol, adorned with garlands of gold beads, jewels, silver bells and silk banners.

To his right, his consort, green Sarasvati plays the vina, flooding the air with melodious sound. To his left is his consort, named The Signless, white as the full moon of compassion: in her hands in angeli at her heart, she holds the stem of a white lotus in full bloom. At its center stands the crystal sword of omniscience. They traverse across the sky amid celestial palaces and offering devis. They are surrounded by rainbows of light which are every kind of knowing.

This great sovereign is the complete spontaneous and ever-present power of wisdom, the deathless Ashe, the inseparability of space and awareness, the resolution of time and space, the life force essence of all the Imperial Rigden Kings.

Gesar hovers in the sky on the back of the red Garuda and he hears the roaring proclamation of the last Rigden. He feels like he is caught in the very center of a storm, overwhelmed by the thunder. And as the words echo in his head, he sees the events they describe unfold before his eyes.

In the very beginning of this world's time,
Amid the world's vast peaceful seas
The four great and eight lesser continents
Were harmoniously ranged around Mount Meru.
Then the consciousness of all beings
Dwelt in of bodies of pure light.

But with time's slow increase,
Fascinated by compounded phenomena,
Grasping at continuance, beings became ever more solid.
Confidence in the power of egoless action waned.

The three lords of materialism grew in strength
And came to appear to humans as transcendental gods.

Men and women became possessed
By the minds of animals, hungry ghosts and hell beings.
They transformed the world into those realms.

The earth was robbed as an unattended treasure house.
The seas became mere fisheries and middens.
Rivers were dammed and lakes used as farms.
Fire became merely a source of household comfort and mechanical power.
The air was fouled.
Forests and plains were destroyed or cultivated according to human need.
Birds, fish, and animals were hunted, captured, butchered and skinned.
The geography of the earth itself was deformed.

Men and women looked to Gods and Asuras for their salvation and solace.
Only deities who promised man's dominion were supplicated.
Only philosophies seeking exclusive human happiness were pursued.

This brings the time of disputes and poisons.
In the headlong race for material gain,
Civilizations and cultures collapse from within and without.
Nations, villages, and families split apart.
Parent and child, brother and sister, life-long friends
Become indifferent strangers and deceitful thieves.
Parents prostitute their children.
Plagues corrupt love.
Insane murderous tyrants, surrounded by panic-stricken sycophants,
Rule the earth by the power of terror alone.
Power, violence, scheming, and raw possession become the only good.
Famine, disease, and warfare become the only truth.
Nobility, compassion, decency, gentleness, courage are mere words.
The world becomes a burning prison house without solace or liberation.
Drugged hallucinations are the only refuge for the poor,
While wealth and spiritual practice are escapes of the rich.

Beginning then in the time of Rigden Samudravijaya
These faiths and practices assume a single face
In the doctrines of the La-los, Madhumati becomes supreme.

In the following 1700 years, Central Asia, India, China, the Middle East,
And half the entire world falls beneath its sway.

Like the stench of a rotting corpse, the vapors from this world
Will begin to poison the air of Shambhala itself.
The dharma will weaken and half the abhidharma will pass away.

The barbarian La-lo King, Drang Tzi Lodro
Will unite his forces in Central India.
Then hearing of Shambhala, seeing it in the smoke of incense,
And incited by the words of his rapacious queen,
He will mass his armies.
Like a maddened elephant, he will press to conquer
All the worlds beyond his own.

Then, suddenly as the sun appears in the eye of a black hurricane,
The Rigden Raudracakrin will appear, filling the whole of the sky.

Because he is the essence of peace
And his mind does not move from the equanimity of dharmata,
Because he is inseparable from the minds
Of the three great protectors of all beings,
He will appear in the shining fortress that Mara cannot destroy.
In the blazing light of spontaneous wisdom
Ordinary insight shall become supreme insight,
The radiant, primordial, changeless free expanse, the completion of time.

For those who cling to the shadow-phenomena of materialism,
And to their proud, cruel and deceptive leaders,
The Rigden Raudracakrin shall appear
As the wrathful sun of reality,
Consuming their path and their very life.

Hosts of Gods who protect the world,
Now magnetized by the pure light of wisdom,
Armies of Asuras who uphold the noble path of warriorship,
And hordes of humans who long for the true awakened state
Shall rise up and assemble around the world-ending Rigden
Like innumerable flocks of birds rising from the dark earth
Up into the dawn sky.

So when the dharma lord emerges from the city of Kalapa
In the samadhi which is Wind-Horse itself,
Moving freely within the vast space of the ayatanas,
Four armies of six million human warriors shall join him.

The great kings, lords, generals and warriors of the universe
Who spontaneously hold the samaya of the Rigden's view.
Shall emerge to lead their armies:
All in splendid golden armor, all bearing lethal weapons,
Riding in their towering battle-carts, riding on their elephants,
Amid boiling seas of cavalry and foot-soldiers.

Three glittering armies of Asuras shall arise
Ferocious, sharp fanged, awesome, and fearless
They will invade the mountaintops, the earth and seas
To destroy the corrupted malice of demonic possession.

A single vast army of worldly and transcendent deities,
Sworn to dazzle, overwhelm and destroy the roots of ego-fixation,
Shall rise to Rigden Raudracakrin and surround him in the sky.

Lion-headed Vishnu, the all pervading, furious with eyes ablaze,
Shall ride out on the back of a fire-red garuda,
Wielding the wheel from which the cycles spin and the sword that severs
ignorance.

Brahma, lord of space and time,
In his gold and ruby chariot with pennants fluttering,
Shall unleash his golden arrows
Which fill all hearts with the fatal hallucinations of passion and birth.

Shiva, Dark Lord of Rishis, and lord of night and dreams,
Flying on an emerald disc with the sound of thunder rolling across the sky
Shall strike with his trident that penetrates birth, existence and death.

Kumara Skanda, leader of the army of the gods,
Ever youthful with six faces and six arms
Will skim the earth on the back of a blue poison-drinking peacock
That is perched within a vermilion and gold chariot

Drawn by blue and white celestial steeds.
He will shoot his arrows, hurl thunderbolts and spears,
And wield his ax and sword in an awe-inspiring display.

The twin Asvin gods, Nasatya and Dasra, lithe, shining and handsome,
Bringers of harvest and health, famine and plague,
Will destroy the fortunes of the enemy.

Great Ganapati white with six arms and one tusk in his elephant head,
Who binds the minute to the infinite,
Containing all phenomena in his great form,
Will appear in his gold and cinnabar cart floating in the air,
Riding within that on the great blue mouse which is the enjoyment of all,
And destroy all false distinctions with his trumpet's scream.

These shall be the foremost amongst the myriad worldly gods
Who shall protect the great dharma in all the ten directions,
When the last Rigden enters the degenerate world.

As the armies clash, the false protectors of the La-los
Who dwell in clouds, mountains, and streams shall be cut apart.
Their powers of divine illusion will disperse like mist.
The Evil Asura Mara Ritha shall be pierced through the dark side of his head.
The Rigden Raudracakrin shall slay the demonic Asura Mara Mati with his spear.
At that very moment, all the holy images and icons of the La-Los will shatter.

Rash and arrogant, drunk on their own power of violence,
The La-lo leaders shall urge their frightened soldiers on
Even as rank upon rank of their troops are slaughtered,
Crushed under chariot wheels, burned with flames of molten steel,
Pierced with arrows, hacked with swords, crushed under elephants' feet,
They shall be pressed into the slaughter by the men behind.

The carnage will continue unabated for days,
Until the Shambhala General Hanumanda slices the throat
Of the La-lo general with his golden sword.
Then all the leaders of darkness, one by one, shall be struck down.

Finally, the Great Dharma Lord himself,
Leaning down from the back of his sky blue steed,
Shall swing his time-ending spear of meteoric iron in a great arc
And send its razor point down through the skull of the La-lo king.
The life thread of the La-lo King and all his followers
Shall be utterly unwound and none shall remain.

At that time the continuity of non-dharma shall be completely cut off.
No darkness, no shadow shall prevail or remain.

Every form of worldly and transcendent virtue
Shall blaze in its complete perfection.
Every form of ignorance and darkness will be dissolved
All phenomena, all beings, all thought
Will be consumed in blazing light.

Vishnu and his armies together with his enemies
Will burn in vast sheets of red light.
Brahma and his armies together with his antagonists
Will dissolve into a gold sky.
Shiva and his retinue, together with his enemies
Will rise as towering clouds of black light.
Skanda and his armies, together with his opponents
Will shimmer as a great silver light.
The Asvin twins and their retinue, together with their enemies
Will become a pervasive green wind of light.
Ganapati and his chariot, attendants together with their antagonists
Will melt into a radiant blue sky.

All impure realms and all pure realms will merge inseparably
As a swirling disc of rainbow light.

The power and display of immemorial karma shall be utterly exhausted
And resolve into a single all-encompassing field of luminosity.

The radiance of love
Shall consume all of space and time.
The duality of good and evil,
Wisdom and ignorance,
Enlightenment and shadow,

Form and emptiness will vanish
In an instant of utter silence.

All duality shall be encompassed and consumed
In meaning devoid of word, context or implication.

Thus the Kingdom of Shambhala's power
Shall be completely given out,
Its being is expended to the last atom,
Its dharma exhausted
And dispersed throughout the whole of space.

Dissolved in a moment of pure light,
This is the end of the time of Shambhala and of the Imperial Rigden Kings.
For an instant, all the beings in all the realms shall dissolve
In the luminous, empty expanse of complete and unfettered wakefulness.
Their light shall be the beginning of a new golden age.

Thus it was said long ago:
The Imperial Rigden Raudracakrin
Returns to his palace in Kalapa, and from that place,
From the unobstructed union of heaven and earth,
Brings all humankind to the complete Shambhala path.

*

King Gesar resumes his Life in Ling

At that moment, an explosion of white light, like a crashing thunderbolt, detonates on the stage. The cataclysm is total. The audience is stunned, deafened, blinded. And when slowly their senses return, they see that the theater, the shadow screen, the actors, the musicians and dancers have all completely disappeared. The people of Ling find themselves sitting under in the light mist of early morning on the damp ground in a cold, empty field.

Simultaneously, Gesar dreams he is consumed in roaring swirls of rainbow light. He merges into a brilliant gold expanse. He is flooded with a life force that does not have a beginning or end. These words echo throughout his being.

The Buddha has shown the indivisibility
Of body, speech and mind.

Thus the past has no origin.
The present has no origin.
The future has no origin.
Reality is pure, immense, true,
All encompassing,
Inconceivably bright,
Completely free.

So like a warrior entering battle,
Like a dragon diving into a golden lake,
Resolve the ceaseless speed of mind
Which clings to an individual fate.
Plunge, open-eyed into the turbulent ocean of phenomena.
Achieve the imperial mind of the Protector of Life.

Glorious Naropa whose mind is the sky has said:
"All phenomena are, by their nature,
"The seeds of the infinite expanse of reality.
"This presents itself naturally and is not attained.
"The realms of desire, form, and formlessness
"Are the natural radiance of the Awakened State."
Knowing this,
Surrender hope and fear.
Dive into golden sea of phenomena's play.

This is the direct experience of the Bardo of Becoming and of Birth.
This is the empowerment of complete reality of the awakened state,
This is the primordial, self-existing samaya.

Suddenly Gesar wakes. Though weakened, cold and aching, he is again completely himself.

The sun rises through the fog; plains and mountains emerge dimly within the pale gray light. The assembled people of Ling shake themselves, as if waking from a night of dreaming. They are dazed at the scale of the furor they just experienced. They do not know when it ended or what to think at all. Even Todong and his family are, despite themselves, stupefied. For some time, they just sit there. It takes a long time to realize that the theater, the tents, the actors and merchants have really vanished.

The bleak misty morning seems exactly the same as the day Gesar left Ling nine months ago. A smell of moldering leaves and dry grass floats beneath the sharp scent of impending snow. All that has happened between then and now is like a dream. The people of Ling begin to stir and look around. It almost doesn't make sense when, in the distance, they see Kyang Ko Kar Kar grazing quietly next to Gesar's tent.

Sechan Dugmo is the first to understand and with a sharp cry she bolts and begins to run. Tseshang Denma, Odkar Gyaltsen, and the other ministers soon follow her.

Panting, she pushes aside the black felt flap of the tent, and in the light of the sun behind her, she sees Gesar, pale and exhausted, breathing softly, asleep. Somehow he has moved from the funeral tent and returned to her bed. Gesar's face is pale as a winter moon, and smooth as jade. She goes up to him, and his eyelids open suddenly. His eyes glitter like obsidian orbs. His stare is remote from ordinary concerns. Startled, Sechan Dugmo pulls back, but Gesar reaches out, takes her hand and looks at her expressionlessly for a long time; then he smiles.

Gesar feels as if a long fever has finally broken. But as he gazes at Sechan Dugmo, she appears to him exactly as she had when he first met her. She looks willowy, beautiful and glowing with youth; full of an arrogance born from privilege and from ignorance of all the cruel turns that life would take. Then he sees her transform before his eyes into a passionate lover and a devoted wife, then a terrified victim kidnapped by his enemies. He sees her resist this enemy, and then slowly, hopelessly become the enemy's lover. Eventually she falls in love and bears this enemy's child. Gesar returns, kills her second husband and has her child killed as well. She then hates Gesar and fears him, and she despises herself for all she has become. It takes many years before she again feels worthy of this Lion Lord and of herself. And here she stands before him, shocked, frightened and now old. Seeing her in this way, Gesar knows that he too is old. He closes his eyes and falls into a dreamless sleep.

Sechan Dugmo sits by the bed, holding Gesar's hand. Odkar Gyaltsen and the ministers stand by the tent door and weep. Behind them a large crowd gathers in silence. After a time, Sechan Dugmo speaks to the people of Ling.

"The Great Lord has returned to us. Exhausted from his long journey, he now needs rest. For us, this is a time of great joy. Ling is once again itself." People cheer, shout victory chants and cry. They jostle to see into the tent. They slap each other on the back as if they knew all along that Gesar would return. Indeed, because of the strange performance they have just witnessed, they feel they've shared his quest and have never doubted its outcome.

Ignored in the excitement, Todong and his family return quickly to their camp and make hasty preparations for returning to their home on the borders of Ling. Todong is downcast and his expression grim. Aside from the most minimal indications of what has to be done, no one speaks. Even his wife does not nag him this time.

Late that afternoon Gesar wakes. Supported by his wife and his old comrade

Tsashang Denma, he walks to the doorway of the tent. To them, it seemed that his body has become very dense and heavy as if it were made of rock. He looks out on the tan plains of Ling glowing in the pale rose light of dusk. His gaze is like that of a wanderer who has returned after many years to his childhood home, filled with warmth at the sight of familiar things, but astonished at the changes that have occurred. As he eyes the tent in which he had lain in state, the Prime Minister asks; "Should we take it down?" And Gesar nods. But when asked if the crematory stupa should be dismantled, he shrugs and shakes his head.

Off in the distance they notice a large caravan moving quickly away from Ling. It is Todong and his entourage. Then Odkar Gyaltsen asks:

"He has been nothing but your enemy. Why have you never destroyed him?"

Gesar smiles at his heir and whispers hoarsely: " If there were no Todong, there would have been no Gesar." Odkar Gyaltsen looks ever more puzzled, and so, after a while Gesar continues slowly emphasizing each word: "Because of him, I could never rest... at all... and because I never rested, I had to be ... myself."

Some days later, Gesar and Sechan Dugmo go for a walk into the foothills of Ling. The pallid noonday sun glimmers behind the rush of approaching snow clouds, and on the horizon, the mountains are already white with ice. Sechan Dugmo is mired in uncertainty and sadness. She knows she should be happy that her spouse is with her once again but she sees how worn out he is. She cannot help feeling that he will not remain for long. As they stand on a hillside, the far off sounds of herdsmen calling, yaks and cattle lowing, and muffled horses hoofs drifted up to them through the whispers of chilly air rustling in the junipers. But in her sadness, the sounds of daily life seem far away. Then Gesar holds her, looks out on the valley of Ling and the black tents of its people, and sings.

**O infinite expanse
Wearing the four elements and colors,
Moment of becoming,
Place of my birth;**

**O silence singing,
All the moments of my life and end;
O stillness,
Veiled and shimmering,
Spontaneous Dharmata;
O radiance,
Adorned with time
AH AH AH**

Oh Lame,
Your embrace is the Bardo of Death and Luminosity
AH AH AH

Oh Dakiniye,
Your embrace is the Bardo of Becoming and Birthplace
AH AH AH

Oh Rupiniye,
Your embrace is the Bardo of Life, Dream and Meditation
AH AH AH

Oh Kandarohe,
Your embrace is the Bardo of Dharmata.
AH AH AH

Oh fever of life,
I am completely abandoned by you.
I am terrified by you.
I am overwhelmed by you.
I am in love with you.
AH

After a while, he says: "If I did not love you so, I would never have known this." Then, tears pour down his cheeks, and Sechan Dugmo, clinging to him, also begins to cry.

*

A Song of Great Compassion

After that, Gesar often takes long walks. As he passes through the camp on the arm of his oldest friend and minister, Tseshang Denma, people are shocked that he still looks much as he had when they had thought he was dead. His face and body are like dried up leather, and the brocade robe he wears now droops on his emaciated body. They do not want to admit it to themselves but they know his life force cannot sustain him much longer.

One morning, he and Tsashang Denma walk out across a nearby field to a place where a black rock outcropping juts out of the earth. This rock has three edges and rises to a rounded top and in this way looks very like a phurba. They stop and look at it. As his friend waits, he noticed Gesar is weeping. All at once Tseshang Denma realizes that Gesar's knows he will soon die. And at the very same moment, he sees that for Gesar, though this is a source of sadness, it is otherwise of no more concern than taking off one set of clothes and putting on another. Gesar turns, looks into his friend's eyes, and whispers:

"There will be no more golden age." Tsashang Denma is shocked, but Gesar takes his arm and sings:

Separating the domains of inner and outer:
The bardos and realms become solid.
 In the natural union of inner and outer,
The bardos and realms are lights of uninterrupted wakefulness.

The light of unceasing love
Carries us from state to state.
And I, Gesar, O beloved friend,
Will soon dissolve completely.
Soon the stage on which I have played will disappear.

Moving from realm to realm
By awareness, by vision, by love,
In song, in memory, in reality
We will continue
Just as the sun passes through years,
Seasons, night and day,
Through mountains and seas of radiant clouds.

In the inseparable union of inner and outer,
The luminous path of universal love unfurls
Like a rainbow banner in the sky.
There is nothing to lead or follow.
There is nothing finally to realize.
There is no success or failure.
There is no separation.
There is only the victory banner of our radiant love
Shining without limit and without end.

In the state of great compassion,
There is no liberation.

*

A Song of Confidence

Odkar Gyaltsen, Gesar's chosen heir cannot sleep. Throughout the night, he is plagued by sorrow and apprehension. He knows that soon he will have to rule, but he feels utterly unprepared. He can find no solace, but finally just before dawn, he falls into an exhausted slumber. He dreams that he is riding alone across the Northern plains of Ling, when he sees the shadow of an eagle swooping across the ground ahead. He looks up. His father appears to him as often in dreams he has appeared before.

High above him, like a white cloud before a gale, Gesar races across the sky on his prancing horse of wind, Kyang Ko Kar Kar. The white silk pennants on the top of Gesar's crystal helmet flutter and his gold brocade and gold chain mail armor sparkle and flash. He holds his crystal sword aloft in his right hand and his antelope bow and arrows in their snow-leopard quiver rest at his left shoulder. In the crook of his left arm is a white victory banner adorned with rainbow tassels arching like a bridge of light.. Odkar Gyaltsen is overwhelmed with longing and a sense of his own weakness. "How, how can I ever follow you?" he thinks in despair.

Fast as a thought, Gesar swoops down, seizes the bridle of Odkar Gyaltsen's horse, and lifts him up into the sky. Then the earth with its mountains and seas and the heavens, and the sun and moon and stars unfurl beneath them like a great carpet, Gesar sings this song of confidence called

The Red Garuda's Cry Which Calls the Spontaneous Presence of the Rigden Kings.

O Imperial Drala of all Dralas, Rigden Lord of Life,
You are primordial existence.
You hold in your left hand the crystal mirror,
The living alaya.
KI

O Imperial Drala of Dralas, Rigden Lord of Life,
You are primordial aspiration.
In your right hand, you brandish a crystal sword,
The inner nature of the seventh consciousness.
SO

O Imperial Drala of Dralas, Rigden Lord of Life,
You are primordial power.
You wear the blazing golden armor of life
And the snow-white pennants on your helmet crackle in the wind
You are the life of the six senses.
A La La

Descend now on the swirling Mu Cord
Which rises from our offering of longing.

Now with your shining blade,
Slash like lightning
Through the clouds of confused desires, doubts and calculation,
Which distort and veil the splendor of your pure domain.

Riding on the great horse of moving space itself,
Releasing and binding the elements and space
With your true command like a roar of thunder,
Show the fearless Tiger of the living seas,
The all-conquering Lion of the living wind,
The deathless Garuda of the living fire,
And the sovereign Dragon of the living earth.
Show the true kingdom and true law of Shambhala,

Pure, real, undeluded, and uncontrived nowness.
Show the true Kingdom and true law of Shambhala,
Which is the intrinsic life force of all humanity.
Swiftly, swiftly, please do this now.
KI KI SO SO ASHE LHA GYEL LO TAK SENG KHYUNG DRUK
DI YAR KYE
KI KI SO SO ASHE LHA GYEL LO TAK SENG KHYUNG DRUK
DI YAR KYE
KI KI SO SO ASHE LHA GYEL LO TAK SENG KHYUNG DRUK
DI YAR KYE

O Rigden Father, in this faithless time
Please remain with us here and do not depart.
Remain here, moving on the pathways of virtue.
Remain here, resting on the raging flames of existence.
Remain here, sustained by the flesh and blood of men and horses.
Remain here, subduing the fears and delusions of all the realms.
Remain here as the only sovereign and law.
Please remain by day and night and sing to us on waking and in dreams.

*

Calling on the Great Four-Armed Mahakala

Odkar Gyaltsen wakes to find it is already noon. His mind is clear and sharp but he feels utterly alone even as the world sparkles and is overwhelmingly alive.

Gesar, King of Ling announces that, in a week's time, he will leave on a final retreat. He calls his people together to speak to them at a last great feast.

Although the sun is gold and bright in a deep cloudless sky, the air is chilly. Cook fires for roasting haunches of meat and keeping pots of stew boiling keep everyone warm. All the clans of Ling have assembled around their standards. Banners the colors of the four directions are hung everywhere and pennants adorned with the four dignities snap in the cold winds. Warriors in their most splendid battle armor stand at attention in the four cardinal directions, and flags bearing the Tiger, Lion, Garuda and Dragon standards fly in the intermediate directions.

Gesar sits immobile with eyes closed on a snow lion skin upon a high golden throne. He is dressed in gold brocade and wears his gold chain mail armor, his crystal helmet with its white satin pennants. His crystal sword is unsheathed on his lap and his antelope bow and arrows in their snow-leopard quiver rest at his left shoulder. In his hands joined in meditation hold a crystal vase of immortality. The sight is as dazzling as if Gesar has become a golden statue rather than a living being.

The people of Ling wait before him anxiously. They all feel as if the ground under their feet is shifting. They do not know what will happen now or what the future will bring. Sechan Dugmo draws near the throne and peers up into Gesar's dark expressionless face. Somewhere far off, a child begins to cry, and suddenly, Gesar's eyes snap open. He nods slightly as he put his forefinger to his lips. He looks up into the sky, and in a clear voice that penetrates directly into every heart, he offers this invocation to the great protector:

Calling On The Four Armed Mahakala:
The Vajra Being Of The Awakened State

HUM HUM HUM
KUNA KUNA KUNA

Holding samsara and nirvana in a single grasp,
The Great Wrathful One, the Four Armed Mahakala
Rises implacably from the uncontrived expanse of space.

HUM BHYO HUM
Suddenly, violently, filling the whole of space,
The Supreme Wisdom Protector,
Rages like a world-consuming tornado

Destroying the border of existence and non-existence,
Binding the realms of wisdom and delusion
In the molten iron whirlwind of his form.
He is the guardian of the path of the awakened state
And his form is the path itself.

HOH
You are smoky black,
The color of a towering thundercloud.
Sheets of lightning flash through your body.
Your three bloodshot eyes encompass the three times.
Your flaming hair and eyebrows are the flickerings of thought.
Your bronze fangs twitch and click together in every secret fear.
Your lips are red with the dark heart's blood of hope.
None can escape you.
You are the nakedness of perception,
The unelaborated ground of wakefulness.

HA HA TA TA
Your laughter, like a crack of lightning, fills the whole of space.
Terror paralyzes all conceptual schemes
And strips them into nakedness.
You bind the pure and impure realms
In the one taste of all phenomena,
You bind all beings to the path of innate compassion.

HUM HUM PHAT
Because of you, we cannot escape the claustrophobia of noise and chaos.
Because of you, we cannot escape the cries of love and suffering,
We see and smell corpses and fresh grass, the lover's touch, the knife's cut.
Because of you, we cannot escape the wakeful state.

Naked enlightenment, free from identity,
Your dance embraces all existence and non-existence,
With your crown of five dried skulls,
The exhausted aspirations of enlightenment;
A necklace of fifty-one human skulls,
The exhausted intentions of the phenomenal world;
You are adorned with the six realms
As jeweled silk scarves, ornaments of bone,

Garlands of flowers and bells,
And a fresh tiger skin round your waist.
Your four arms are the four directions.
In your first right hand, you hold a hooked knife.
In your lower right hand, a burning sword.
In your first left hand at your heart, you hold a kapala,
And you brandish the vajra khatvanga in your lower left hand.
In every action, you bind the ignorant and deluded
To the vibrant and unsparing life of wakefulness.

You are the natural state which none can escape,
The truth none can refute,
The samaya none can violate.
When doubt and uncertainty
Night, confusion, dark and fear
Come to us
Who wanderer on the path of impermanence;
May we see the vivid face of the awakened state
May we see this,
Your face.
Hold us in your scalding heart,
And do not let us part.
HA HA HUM HUM
HUM BHYO HUM

This chant makes the sky shake and every atom of the mountains and plains shiver. All thoughts are paralyzed and no one moves. Then Gesar bursts out laughing, and calls for something to drink. Suddenly it is just like the great victory feasts of years ago. Everyone is giggling, and gossiping and children are racing underfoot everywhere. Barrels of rice wine are opened. Round after round toasting the sovereign, his prowess, his wife, his heir, his ministers and generals, his warriors, his horse, his land begins.

*

The Offering of Basic Goodness.

Later as twilight falls, one by one the people of Ling approach the throne to receive Gesar's blessing. He smiles at each and speaks to some. But as they leave, each comes away feeling that this was not a welcoming, but a farewell, and that soon they will see Gesar no more.

Finally Gesar stands to address his people, and a hush fell. Soon, he tells them, he will be going to White Mountain Cave for a final retreat with a few of his heart companions. Then in a dry voice that sounds like the scraping of dry leaves on a cold ground, he sings:

This is the end of our time together.
Hesitation, depression, fear and doubt are ended.
The panoply of life and death is seen to its depth.
You have seen that outer and inner battles do not cease.
You have seen the wakefulness that does not cease.
This is the offering of basic goodness.
Whatever happens in your life
Is worthy of being your path.

And with that Gesar raises a toast to all of them. He thanks them for their loyalty, their exertions, and their love. "Without you I would not have lived," he tells them, and everyone begins to cry. Then abruptly Gesar returns to his tent.

Two weeks later, in the White Mountain Cave that looks out across rank upon rank mountain ranges, rivers and valleys veiled in coils of clouds, Gesar, King and Lion Lord of Ling, the King of All Warriors leaves this world.

It is said that at that same instant a pulse of brilliant white light fills the sky erasing even the light of the sun and the moon. And it is likewise said that throughout the world, though some experience this as the sight of a deity, some as a sudden shock, some as a sudden joy, some as death, some as a sneeze, for an instant, the mind of every living being stops.

And then continues as Gesar himself continues, for, as is said:

Out of the ground of longing and invocation, Gesar here remains.
Out of the path of story, Gesar here continues.
Out of chaos and fear, Gesar here wakes,
Out of the completion of song,
Gesar is now welded in our hearts.
So in these forms, as Protector, Yidam, and Guru,
Gesar now lives.
Here and now,
He offers himself to you.

*

COLOPHON

May the heart transmission of the teachings of the Imperial Rigden Father
And of his only heart son, the Dorje Dradul of Mukpo Dong
Flow like a luminous river lighting every heart
In all the galaxies of stars.

ChodzinPaden
Magyel Pomra Sayi Dakpo

GLOSSARY

Abhisheka: (lit. sprinkling or anointing) Ceremony of empowerment enabling the recipient to do certain practices and reach certain kinds of attainment. There are four empowerments relating to body, speech, mind, and their essence.

Acarya: (lit. teacher) Title given to certain lineage holders.

Amrita: (lit: anti-death) That which sustains beyond life and death; that which intoxicates conventional views.

Ashe: (lit. primordial stroke) The stroke that cuts through doubt, and aggression towards self and other.

Bhagavan: blessed one

Bhumipala: Earth Protector

Bindu: (lit: dot or point) mind essence

Buddha: (lit. the awakened one)

Co-emergence: simultaneity of wisdom and ignorance

Dakini: (lit: sky-goer) wrathful or semi-wrathful female deity embodying co-emergent wisdom

Dharma: (lit. law or truth) usually here the Buddhist teachings, but may in other contexts refer to normative teachings of other kinds.

Dharmadhatu: (space of phenomena) all encompassing space

Drala: (lit. above enemy) The worldly and transcendent power inherent in direct perception of phenomena. The worldly dralas are the specific communicative nature of sky, mountains, earth, water and the underground.

EVAM: Union of prajna and upaya, wisdom and method.

Garuda: Mythical Indian Bird that is fully-grown on emerging from the egg, thus a symbol of the awakened mind.

Heruka: (lit. blood drinker) wrathful male embodiment of wisdom flourishing in whatever circumstances he finds himself.

Jnana: Wisdom, spontaneous presence

Kalapa: The capitol city of the Kingdom of Shambhala

Kapala: skull cup

Karma: (lit. action) the continuum of cause and effect, action and result

Kaya: (lit. body) form, as in the three bodies or forms of the Buddha: Dharmakaya (body or form of truth); Sambhogakaya (body or form of enjoyment); and Nirmanakaya (emanation body as manifest in physical form).

Ki and So: The syllables of the warrior cry bring down the power of Drala and Werma

Lungta: (lit. wind horse) The basic energy of wakefulness.

Mahamudra: (lit. Great Seal). A lineage of meditative traditions in which all experiences are realized in their essential nature as joining prajna and skillful means. Here the vividness of experience is spontaneously realized as the luminous display of the deity.

Mahasiddha: (lit great accomplished one) An accomplished lineage master.

Nadi: The inner pathways of the body through which the bindu moves.

Naga: Serpents, dragons and those treasure holders who dwell beneath the earth or sea.

Padma Sambhava: The great Indian teacher, regarded as the second Buddha, who brought Tantric Buddhism to the Himalayas

Phurba: three bladed dagger which penetrates passion, aggression and ignorance

Prajna: (lit. highest knowledge) the natural precision of awareness that penetrates all dualistic obstacles.

Prana: (lit. wind) inner energy by which the bindu moves through the nadis.

Rigden: The Title of the rulers of Shambhala

Rigpa: Ceaseless primordial awareness, the basic awareness that underlies and continues through all mental states, sleeping, wakefulness, life and death

Samadhi: (lit: absorption or concentration) sometimes a synonym for meditation.

Samsara: The endless cycle of painful illusion caused by ignorance, grasping and fixation.

Shambhala: An enlightened society in the human realm.

Shamatha: (lit. Taming or calming the mind) Letting the mind rest in the space in which thoughts arise, dwell, and decay.

Siddha: one who has siddhi

Siddhi: An aspect of realization in which the inseparability of relative and absolute reality manifest as power over apparent phenomena..

Sugatagharba: As in Tathagathagharba, innate enlightenment, but here the emphasis is on its experiential component.

Sunyata: (lit. emptiness) The realization that self and other are merely temporary and insubstantial constructs, and that reality itself is completely free from any kind of conceptual or emotional biases.

Tathaghatagharba: (lit. Buddha nature) Intrinsic complete natural wakefulness

Tilopa: The 10th Century Indian Mahasiddha who received the Mahamudra teachings directly from primordial awareness itself and passed them down in the lineages that became today the Kagyupa.

Upaya: (skillful means) The methods by which the inner realization of the lineage is conveyed.

Vajra: (lit. thunderbolt) a ritual object in the form of a five or none pointed thunderbolt that symbolizes the indestructible nature of wisdom and the awakened state.

Vajrayogini: The great dakini who is the essence of co-emergence and the principal of the natural transformation of ignorance and passion into wisdom and skillful means.

Vajrasattva: (lit. Vajra being) The principal of the innate purity if the awakened state.

Vipassana: (insight) That aspect of meditation that relates to mind as motion (as distinct from Shamatha which relates to the unmoving aspect); clear seeing into the patterns of mind and phenomena.

Werma: Lineage of ancestral protectors who particularly ensure prosperity.

Yidam: A deity through which the practitioner uncovers her or his own awakened nature.

Yogi: male practitioner

Yogini: female practitioner

ACKNOWLEDGEMENTS

This book would not have come into its present form without the ongoing encouragement and frequent hard work of Helen Berliner, Christine Cooper, the late Susan Edwards, Louisa Ermelino, Meg Federico, Martin Fritter, Kenneth Green, Genny Kapular, the Venerable Khandro Rinpoche, Peter Lieberson, Gianni Longo, David McCarthy, Larry Mermelstein, Julie Nowick, Rutger Penick, Sir John Perks OLK, the late Del Riddle, Ed and Deb Shapiro, Pamela Sichel, Kidder Smith, the Venerable Tulku Thondup, Eve Wallace, David Warren, James Yensan and Jenny Young. I apologize to any I have neglected to mention here, but I'm indebted to you all.

CPSIA information can be obtained at www.ICGtesting.com
Printed in the USA
LVOW10s1056070116

PP10438600001B/2/P